IGNACIO RAMONET is the editor of *Le Monde diplomatique,* a French monthly newspaper published in several languages and with an international circulation of one million copies. He is founder and president of French ATTAC, a key organization in the antiglobalization movement and the World Social Forum. A professor of media studies at the University of Paris VII, Ramonet is the author of several books about the media and geopolitics.

WARS OF THE 21ˢᵗ CENTURY

NEW THREATS NEW FEARS

IGNACIO RAMONET

TRANSLATED BY JULIE FLANAGAN

Ocean Press
Melbourne ■ New York
www.oceanbooks.com.au

Cover design by Sean Walsh and ::maybe

ISBN 1-876175-96-6
Library of Congress Control No: 2003113380

First Printed in Australia 2004

Published by Ocean Press

Australia: GPO Box 3279, Melbourne, Victoria 3001, Australia
Fax: (61-3) 9329 5040 Tel: (61-3) 9326 4280
E-mail: info@oceanbooks.com.au

USA: PO Box 1186, Old Chelsea Stn., New York, NY 10113-1186, USA
Tel: (718) 756 5586

Ocean Press Distributors:

United States and Canada: **Consortium Book Sales and Distribution**
Tel: 1-800-283-3572   www.cbsd.com

Australia and New Zealand: **Palgrave Macmillan**
E-mail: customer.service@macmillan.com.au

Britain and Europe: **Pluto Books**
E-mail: pluto@plutobooks.com

Cuba and Latin America: **Ocean Press**
E-mail: oceanhav@enet.cu

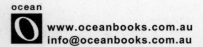

ocean
www.oceanbooks.com.au
info@oceanbooks.com.au

CONTENTS

For my mother †,
fighter for social rights
For my father,
combatant in the Spanish Civil War

THE NEW FACE OF THE WORLD

Two years on from the attacks of September 11, 2001, in the wake of the recent Iraq war and the war against the al-Qaida terrorist network and the Taliban regime, what are the main geopolitical characteristics of the planet as we stand at the threshold of the 21st century?

The United States dominates the world as no other empire has ever done. Its supremacy is overwhelming in the five traditional spheres of power: political, economic, military, technological and cultural. One U.S. analyst has stated that, in a sense, the United States is the first "proto-world state" with the capacity to lead a modern universal empire, a spontaneous empire whose members voluntarily submit to its authority.[1]

For the first time in the history of humanity, the world finds itself under the domination of a single hyperpower. In Afghanistan, this hyperpower displayed its imperial hegemony in three ways: by wiping out in a matter of weeks the Taliban regime and the majority of the al-Qaida armed networks that supported it; by setting up a formidable diplomatic coalition in support of this act of reprisal (particularly with the contributions of Russia and China) while simultaneously limiting any reference to the United Nations to a bare minimum; and finally, by recruiting the once-proud British forces as mere auxiliary troops, while holding at arm's length obliging but nonessential allies such as France, Germany, Spain, Italy, Canada and Japan.

In this new era, however, such a display of military and diplomatic might is deceptive. Despite its immense superiority and the fact that the enterprise would have faced no technological difficulties in doing so, the United States did not consider pressing home its advantage to complete the conquest and occupation of Afghanistan. England had tried to do so in the 19th century, as had Russia in the 20th. Why not the United States? In contrast to previous engagements of the 19th and 20th centuries, military supremacy is no longer understood in terms of territorial conquest. In the present circumstances, and particularly when considered over the long term, this is a politically uncontrollable, militarily dangerous and economically ruinous exercise. In a context where the mass media has become a strategic actor of prime importance, it is the kiss of death.[2]

THE DYNAMICS OF GLOBALIZATION

Another crucial phenomenon: all states are affected by the dynamics of globalization, in a kind of second capitalist revolution. Economic globalization has spread to the most remote corners of the planet, irrespective of the independence of peoples or the diversity of governmental regimes.

This process is so widespread that the world is experiencing a new period of conquest comparable with the colonial period. If, however, the leading actors in the previous victorious expansion were states, this time around the would-be conquerors of the world are private enterprises and industrial and financial conglomerates. The lords of the Earth have never been so few or so powerful. These groups are concentrated in the United States-European Union-Japan triad. Half of them are based in the United States.

This concentration of capital and power has accelerated at an incredible rate over the last 20 years, due to the revolution in information technology. The newborn 21st century will witness another qualitative leap, thanks to modern genetic techniques to manipulate life. The privatization of the human genome and the generalized concession of patents on biological processes are opening up new prospects for capitalist expansion. Large-scale privatization of all that affects life and nature is underway, favoring the appearance of the most absolute power history has ever known.

Globalization is less concerned with conquering countries than with acquiring markets. The aim of modern power is no longer the annexation of territory, as in the times of the great invasions or colonial expansion, but the control of wealth. The conquest is accompanied by huge devastation, as was witnessed in the spectacular crash of Argentina in December 2001. That country was the principal example of the much-vaunted universal model that the International Monetary Fund (IMF), with dogmatic obstinacy, has tried to export throughout the world. The fall of Argentina is to neoliberalism what the fall of the Berlin Wall was to state socialism: evidence of discredit, confirmation of failure. In every corner of the globe entire industrial sectors are heading for shutdown, with all the social suffering this entails: massive unemployment, underemployment, scarcity and exclusion. In the European Union alone, there are 18 million unemployed; around the world, a billion unemployed and underemployed. The overexploitation of men, women and, most scandalous of all, children, continues: 300 million minors are victims of such brutal treatment.

Globalization also means the plundering of nature: pillage on a planetary scale. Large private companies ravage the environment using methods that are beyond the pale; they harvest natural resources that are the common property of all humanity for their own gain; and they do it without scruples and with nothing to hinder them. This phenomenon is accompanied by criminal economics, linked to the world of finance and the big banks who recycle sums of over a trillion euros per year,[3] or more than the Gross National Product (GNP)[4] of one third of humanity.

UNGOVERNABLE CHAOTIC ENTITIES

This generalized commercialization has drastically exacerbated inequality. While world production of basic foodstuffs provides 110 percent of the planet's needs, 30 million people continue to die of hunger each year and more than 800 million suffer from malnutrition.

In 1960, the world's richest 20 percent earned more than 30 times as much as the poorest 20 percent. This was a scandalous situation yet rather than improving, it continues to worsen: at present, the earnings of the richest group are 82 times higher than those of the poor. Of the world's six billion inhabitants, 500 million live in comfort, while 5.5 billion live in conditions of want. The world is traveling down the wrong path.

State structures, like traditional social structures, have been swept aside with catastrophic consequences. All around the world, in the South and the East, the state is falling apart. Authorities have withdrawn or have been expelled from peripheral areas, which then become completely lawless. In Pakistan, the Caucasus, Algeria, Somalia, Sudan, the Congo, Colombia, the Philippines and Sri Lanka, chaotic and ungovernable entities have appeared, dispensing with any form of legality and representing a return to barbarism. Force prevails over law and only violent groups are capable of making citizens submit to their imposed law.

New threats are emerging: hyperterrorism, religious or ethnic fanaticism, nuclear proliferation, organized crime, mafia networks, financial speculation, the collapse of huge companies (Enron), corruption on a grand scale, the spread of new pandemics (AIDS, the Ebola virus, Creutzfeld-Jakob Disease), ecological disasters, the greenhouse effect, desertification, etc.

Just when democracy and freedom are seemingly triumphing in a world that has rid itself of its worst dictatorial regimes, censorship and different kinds of manipulation have returned, in different guises, with a paradoxical vengeance. We are seductively offered the promise of a kind of "brave new world," which distracts citizens and aims to keep them out of civic and political activities. In these new times of alienation, the era of the internet, a single world culture or "global culture," information technology — the new "opiate of the masses" — is playing a fundamental ideological role in gagging thought.

These structural and conceptual changes which began a decade ago have caused nothing less than a worldwide explosion. Basic geopolitical concepts such as the state, power, sovereignty, independence, borders and democracy have acquired totally new meanings, and to such an extent that if we look at the actual functioning of international life we cannot fail to notice that the leading actors have changed.

On a planetary scale, the three main actors (who under the monarchical *ancien régime* were the nobility, the clergy and the third estate) are currently (1) associations of states: NAFTA (the United States, Canada and Mexico), the European Union, Mercosur, ASEAN, etc.; (2) transnational companies and the huge media and finance groups; and (3) NGOs of global influence (Greenpeace, Amnesty International, ATTAC, Human Rights Watch, World Wildlife Fund for Nature etc.). These three new actors operate in a global framework that is determined — and this is a sign of the times — not so much by the United Nations as by the World Trade Organization (WTO), the new world arbiter.

The democratic vote of the citizens generally signifies little in the internal functioning of these three main agencies. This great mutation of the world, which has removed any meaning from democracy, has occurred without anyone really noticing it, not even the politicians who were apparently in charge.

COMBATING NEOLIBERAL GLOBALIZATION

In fact, these swift and brutal changes have destabilized the political leaders themselves. Most feel overwhelmed by the advent of a globalization which has changed the rules of the game and reduced them, at least partially, to impotence. The true lords of the Earth are not those who flaunt the trappings of political power. This is why citizens have multiplied their activities and mobilizations against the new rulers, as we saw in December 1999 with the WTO summit in Seattle, and subsequently in Prague, Davos, Nice, Quebec, Genoa and Barcelona. They are convinced that the fundamental aim of neoliberal globalization in this new millennium is the destruction of collective initiative and an appropriation of the public and social spheres by the market and private sector. They are determined to resist.

In the era of neoliberalism, geopolitical supremacy and the actions of the hyperpower have proven incapable of guaranteeing a satisfactory level of human development for all citizens. Among the inhabitants of a country as rich as the United States, for example, are 32 million people whose life expectancy is less than 60 years; 40 million without medical cover; 45 million living below the poverty line; and the figure for functional illiteracy is 52 million. Similarly, in the heart of the opulent European Union, there are 50 million poor and 18 million unemployed.

On a worldwide level, poverty continues to be the rule and welfare the exception. The different forms of inequality have become a structural feature of our times. They continue to worsen, creating an ever-widening gulf between rich and poor. The 225 greatest fortunes in the world represent a total of over a trillion euros, or the equivalent of the earnings of the poorest 47 percent of the world's population (2.5 billion human beings!). Today there are individuals who are richer than many states: the sum total of the wealth of the 15 richest people in the world is greater than the GNP of all the sub-Saharan African countries.

DOMINATORS AND DOMINATED

Who dominates the world at the threshold of the 21st century? It could be claimed that the planet is in the hands of a double triumvirate which acts as a kind of world executive. In the geopolitical and military domains, the triumvirate consists of the United States, the United Kingdom and France; the economic sphere is controlled by the United States, Germany and Japan. In both areas, the United

States clearly occupies the most dominant position.

At the beginning of the 20th century, there were some 40 states in the world; that number has now increased to almost 200. The proliferation of states was one of the major features of the 20th century. Yet in the geopolitical sphere, the world is still dominated by the small group of states (the United Kingdom, France, Germany, Japan and the United States) that were already in control at the end of the 19th century. Among the dozens of states that appeared with the breakup of the British, French, Spanish, Dutch, Portuguese and Belgian colonial empires, only three (South Korea, Singapore and Taiwan) have attained a level of progress permitting them to be included in the list of developed countries. The rest are stranded in chronic underdevelopment and seemingly never-ending poverty.

Escaping from this situation will be all the more difficult as their economies depend on the prices they get for raw materials (including fossil fuels). Prices continue to fall, showing no sign of stabilizing, and the biggest developed countries, apart from not wanting to pay a fair price for raw materials, have considerably reduced their usage of a good number of basic products (metals, fibers, foodstuffs), or have replaced them with synthetic materials. In Japan, for example, each unit of industrial production has reduced its consumption of raw materials to almost 40 percent of its usage in 1973.

As the 21st century advances, the new wealth of nations will increasingly be calculated on the basis of knowledge, information, research and the capacity for innovation, rather than the production of raw materials. In this respect, it is no exaggeration to say, in this postindustrial era, that the three traditional trappings of power — territorial expansion, demographic significance and raw material production — are no longer enviable attributes, but, paradoxically, serious liabilities.

The vast, highly populated states that are extremely rich in raw materials — Russia, India, China, Brazil, Nigeria, Indonesia, Pakistan and Mexico — are among the poorest countries in the world. The United States is the exception that confirms the rule. At the other end of the scale, microstates with hardly any territory, very low population and no raw materials — Monaco, Liechtenstein, Gibraltar, the Cayman Islands and Singapore — have some of the highest per capita incomes in the world.

Generalized chaos, akin to a black hole, is constantly expanding, attracting and engulfing an increasing number of states with stagnant economic systems, further swelling the growing number of countries characterized by endemic violence. Since 1989, the year marked by the end of the Cold War, there have been more than 70 armed conflicts, leaving hundreds of thousands dead and over 17 million refugees. In many parts of the globe, modern daily life is simply infernal. It is hardly surprising that a growing number of people, especially younger people, want to escape from the chaos and violence and attempt to emigrate, whatever the price, to the developed and pacified zones of Western Europe and North America.

In many poor countries of the South, the state has failed. It has proven itself unable to guarantee peace, development and security to its citizens, who are then obliged to emigrate in huge numbers. About 120,000 Moroccans, for example, emigrate each year, most of them illegally. Six million Moroccans already live in other countries, that is to say, one out of every five Moroccans. This proportion of emigrants is much higher than in the European countries that headed the emigration figures in the 19th and 20th centuries: Ireland, Italy, Poland, Portugal and Spain. It is the case that, in some underdeveloped countries, inhabitants have disowned the struggle of their predecessors for independence and are now calling for a return of the colonial power (the Comoro Islands and France) or even pure and simple absorption by the dominant metropolis (Puerto Rico and the United States). The Third World has ceased to exist as a political entity.

At a time when the second capitalist revolution, the globalization of the economy and technological developments are changing the geopolitical panorama, there are several other symptoms of the crisis of the nation-state and politics. Moreover, the number of macro-companies, frequently with more muscle than states, is multiplying with takeovers and mergers. The turnover of General Motors is greater than the GNP of Denmark, while that of Exxon Mobil exceeds Austria's. Each of the top 100 transnational companies sells more than the total exports of any of the 20 poorest countries. These global macro-companies dominate 70 percent of the world's trade.

Their leaders, like those of the large finance and media groups, are the people who are truly in power. Through their influential lobbies, they bring all their weight to bear on decisions made by legitimate governments and their elected parliaments. In short, they have hijacked democracy for their own ends.

Traditional countervailing powers (political parties, unions, free press), while more necessary than ever before, seem to have little influence. Now that we are bound by the 21st century private contract, citizens are wondering what bold initiatives might reestablish the social contract. They remember that in October 1917, the Bolshevik Revolution took only 10 days to "shake the world." For the first time, the capitalist steamroller was stopped in its tracks for a lengthy period.

The thrust of capitalism benefited from the contributions of great theorists (Adam Smith, David Ricardo), decisive technological advances (the steam engine, railway) and major geopolitical transformations (the consolidation of the British Empire, the 1871 unification of Germany, the emergence of the United States). The combined effect of all these factors brought about the first capitalist revolution. Yet, at the same time, this phenomenon crushed the very workers whose efforts in the new factories were creating the wealth, as the disturbing novels of Charles Dickens, Émile Zola and Jack London testify. How would it be possible to take collective advantage of the formidable wealth being produced by industrialization, and therefore avoid the social annihilation of the poor?

Karl Marx would respond to this question in his fundamental work *Capital* (1867). Fifty years more would have to pass before the brilliant political strategist Lenin came to power as leader of the Bolsheviks, founding the Soviet Union with the messianic hope of freeing the "proletariat of the world."

THE SECOND CAPITALIST REVOLUTION

Eighty years later, the Soviet Union was in tatters and the planet was experiencing another great mutation that I have called here the "second capitalist revolution." Like the first, this was the result of the convergence of a number of transformations that have occurred in three fields. First: the technological sphere. Computerization of all sectors of activity, combined with the digital revolution have brought the advent of information highways (sound, text and images transmitted at the speed of light). This has gone hand-in-hand with revolutionary changes in the domains of work, the economy, communication, education, procreation, leisure, etc.

Second: the economic sphere. The new technologies have favored the expansion of the financial sphere and have stimulated activities with four essential characteristics: they are global, permanent, immediate and immaterial in nature. The big bang of the stock exchanges and the deregulation pushed by Margaret Thatcher and Ronald Reagan in the 1980s fuelled the globalization of the economy. This constitutes the fundamental dynamic of this new century and no country can be free of it.

Third: the sociological sphere. The two transformations mentioned above have ridden roughshod over the traditional prerogatives of the nation-state and have invalidated certain concepts of political representation and power. Once hierarchical, vertical and authoritarian, power today has taken on an apparently horizontal and — thanks to the manipulation of people's awareness by the mass media — consensual structure. Shocked and disoriented by these tremendous changes, societies are now throwing themselves into a desperate quest for meaning and viable social models.

Simultaneously, two of the mainstays of modern democracy, progress and social cohesion, have been replaced by two alternatives — communication and the market — that undermine its very nature.

Communication, today's number one fetish, is presented as a means of regulating everything, including interpersonal conflicts within the family, school, business, the factory or the state. It is the universal pacifier. Nonetheless, it is reasonable to fear that its very abundance is giving rise to a new form of alienation, and that its excesses, rather than liberating consciousness, end up imprisoning it.[5]

The market today tends to manage and regulate all human activities. Once, certain areas of life — culture, sport and religion — were beyond its reach. Now they have been absorbed into the market sphere. Governments are gradually handing over public-sector activities (power, railways, postal services, education etc.) to the market through privatization.

Yet the market is still the main enemy of social and worldwide cohesion as its essential logic only conceives of a society divided into two groups: the solvent and the non-solvent. The latter, those who neither produce nor consume, are of no interest whatsoever. They are not, shall we say, part of the game. By its very nature, the market is a producer of inequalities, no impediment to its exhibiting an astonishing arrogance.

This anecdote is sufficiently revealing: some time ago, an advertisement appeared on the walls of dozens of airport passageways throughout Europe. Imitating the graphic style of the images of the Chinese Cultural Revolution, it showed a row of smiling demonstrators advancing at the head of a march, their multicolored flags waving in the wind as they shouted, "Capitalists of the world, unite!" This was a *Forbes* advertisement, the U.S. millionaires' magazine, and a parody of the famous communist slogan "Proletarians of the world, unite!" The ad was the magazine's ironic way of commemorating the 150th anniversary of *The Communist Manifesto*, written by Karl Marx and Friedrich Engels, the 1848 French Revolution (which brought in universal male suffrage and the abolition of slavery), and the Paris student uprisings in May 1968. It was also a way of asserting, with no fear of retaliation (the posters were not ripped, smudged, scribbled on or "jammed"), two things: communism is no longer a threat and capitalism is on the offensive. How can we explain this new arrogance of capital?

A DREAM SHATTERED

The fall of the Berlin Wall and the disappearance of the Soviet Union gave way to an atmosphere of political stupefaction — symptomatic of mourning the loss of a dream. The sudden revelations of the consequences of decades of state ownership in the East profoundly shocked the conscience of the world. This system, with neither individual freedoms nor a market economy, was revealed in all its tragic absurdity and concomitant injustice. Socialist thought seemed to collapse for good at that point, as did the paradigm of progress as an ideology aspiring to a complete plan for the future with a mathematical programming of happiness.

Four new convictions took shape among the left, conditioning the hope to radically transform society: (1) no country could develop in any serious way without a market economy; (2) systematic nationalization of the means of production and trade only resulted in waste and penury; (3) austerity in the service of equality did not constitute a government program in itself; (4) a necessary condition of freedom of thought and expression is a certain degree of economic freedom.

The failure of communism and the retreat of socialism have rebounded to cause an ideological dismantling of the traditional right (whose functional base was anticommunism) and enshrined neoliberalism as the great victor in the East-West confrontation. With its wings clipped at the start of the 20th century, neoliberalism has now seen the disappearance of its main adversaries and is spreading across the globe with many times its former energy. It dreams of imposing its own worldview, its own value system, its own utopia, the world over.

This enterprise of conquest is called "globalization." It is the result of greater interdependence of all national economies, tied to the totally free circulation of capital, the suppression of tariff barriers and regulations and intensified free trade exchange, as advocated by the World Bank, the IMF, the Organization for Economic Cooperation and Development (OECD) and the WTO. A rupture has occurred between the finance economy and the real economy. Of the almost €1.5 trillion that represent daily financial transactions on a world scale, only one percent is devoted to the creation of new wealth. The rest is speculative.

The spectacular rise of neoliberalism has been accompanied, even in the more developed countries, by a significant decline in the role of public actors, beginning with the parliaments. There has also been a notable increase in ecological spoliation, inequality, poverty and unemployment, bringing with it the associated social consequences: an explosion of violence, delinquency and insecurity. These consequences represent the negation of the modern state and of citizenship.

We are also witnessing a radical dissociation between the evolution of new technologies, on the one hand, and the notion of social progress on the other. Advances in molecular biology since the early 1960s, combined with the calculating power presently offered by computer science, have shattered the general stability of the technical system and proven that public powers are increasingly out of their depth. The result: politicians, those who are supposed to be responsible for the governing of their citizens, are incapable of gauging the threats that this technological acceleration poses to the future of humanity.[6] Once again, the crucial decisions are made by nonelected experts who have not consulted the citizens and have dictated government policies from behind the scenes.

THE FUTURE OF HUMANITY

Seen from afar, planet Earth is beautiful with its blue raiment, its cottony white smattering of clouds and the impression of opulence and wealth it conveys with its luxuriant vegetation, exuberant flowers and abundant fauna. For millennia, generous nature reigned, and since our first appearance on Earth, humanity has been nourished by and has lived in symbiosis with it.

Nonetheless, since the latter half of the 19th century and the Industrial Revolution, humanity seems to have been bent on systematically destroying the natural environment in the name of progress and development. The land, waters and atmosphere of the planet have fallen victim to all manner of devastation. Galloping urbanization, the logging of tropical forests, the contamination of seas and rivers, global warming, the thinning of the ozone layer, acid rain... Pollution endangers the future of our planet.

In addition, human beings now have the ability to genetically modify the species itself. The scientific adventure is gathering ground, and can now offer a glimpse of the time when for some, cloning will be a reasonable option. Yet acceptable limits are still to be fixed, on both the national and the international scale. The birth of Dolly in the spring of 1997, the cloned sheep that survived into maturity, provided definitive proof for anyone who doubted the possibility. Similarly, the arrival of genetically manipulated products such as corn and soybeans on the European market raises many questions about possible risks. Who has developed these genetically modified organisms (GMOs) and with what aim? Was it sensible? Was it really necessary?

By mid-2003, half the world's population could be faced with a serious lack of drinking water. In 2010, the globe's forest cover will have diminished by 40 percent in comparison to 1990. In 2025, the world's population is expected to reach between 7.5 billion and 9.5 billion inhabitants, in comparison to the six billion of today. By 2040, the accumulation of greenhouse gases could have caused an increase of between one and two degrees centigrade of the average temperature of the planet, and a rise in sea level of between 0.2 and 1.5 meters.

Both industrialized nations — whose prosperity is largely based on excessive production and overexploitation of the environment — and the developing world, will have to work swiftly to find a response to our present need, without, however, jeopardizing the capacity of future generations to satisfy theirs.

What are the main challenges faced by humanity at the start of the 21st century? Preventing the deviations of science, now principally a technoscience which moves ever closer to the market; reducing pollution and combating global climatic change; protecting biodiversity and stopping the depletion of resources; putting an end to soil erosion and desertification; finding a way of feeding between eight and 10 billion human beings.

This out-and-out productivism is the main cause of the current ravaging of natural resources. The proliferation of natural disasters and their associated problems are of growing concern to the world's citizens. The disappearance of many species of flora and fauna is creating disturbing imbalances. Protecting biodiversity and preserving the variety of living creatures through sustainable development has become imperative. The problem of environmental protection has brought the very survival of the human species into question.

The destruction of the environment has long-term consequences and its effects may be irreversible. To give one example: it will take centuries, if not millennia, for some types of nuclear waste to lose their radioactivity. The planet is being eroded by waste products. On a worldwide scale, two billion tons of solid industrial waste, not including about 350 million tons of hazardous waste, are produced each year. To this must be added the 7,000 tons of nuclear products that we do not know how to dispose of. The OECD countries (in other words, the richest in the world) are responsible for 90 percent of the production of these dangerous waste materials.

The concern to safeguard nature goes back to ancient times, to the writings of ancient Roman agronomists on soil conservation and the first regulations aimed at preventing deforestation because of demographic expansion in the 3rd century AD. Ecological thinking did not really take shape, however, until the beginning of the 20th century.

In 1910, the Swedish chemist Svante Arrhenius was the first to formulate a hypothesis that global warming was linked with the progressive accumulation of industrial gases in the atmosphere.

Other early thinkers such as biologist Vladimir Vernadsky, in 1926, and economist Kenneth Boulding, in the 1950s, were concerned about the impact of human activities on the environment.

After 1970, public opinion began to demonstrate alarm at the long-term consequences that might result from rapid economic and demographic expansion. Works like *Only One Earth*[7] and the 1972 Club of Rome report *The Limits of Growth*[8] fueled fears of a huge ecological catastrophe caused by overpopulation, pollution and depletion of natural resources.

The 1972 Stockholm Conference and the World Conservation Strategy[9] attempted to define the characteristics of sustainable and environmentally friendly development. After being eclipsed during the years of the crisis, the question of "sustainable development" or "ecodevelopment" returned to the fore in 1987 with the publication of the UN report *Our Common Future*.[10]

SCARCITY OF DRINKING WATER

By the 16th century, there were 450 million individuals on Earth; in 1900 there were 1.5 billion, and by 1950 another billion were added. Today, the world's population is growing at an unprecedented rate. Our planet is now home to some 6.3 billion individuals. It is envisaged that this figure will have climbed to about 10 billion by 2050. In 2002, 95 percent of the planet's newcomers were born in developing countries.

If everyone on Earth enjoyed the same standard of living as the Swiss, the planet could barely meet the needs of 600 million people. If, on the other hand, we agreed to live like Bengali peasants, there would be resources available for between 18 and 20 billion people. In the last decade, 100 million people have not had enough firewood to cook two meals a day and, at present, 1.5 billion face the imminent threat of not having enough to cook and keep warm. It has been calculated that 800 million people are suffering from malnutrition.

The scarcity of water on the planet is equally disturbing. Water will inevitably become the source of social and economic tensions that might eventually lead to war. North Africa and the Middle East are the most affected regions. According to expert predictions, the water available per capita will have diminished by 80 percent in a period equivalent to one human lifetime. Between 1960 and 2025, it will have dropped from 3.45 million liters per person to 667,000 liters.

There are many threats to fresh water resources. Rerouting rivers for irrigation causes the rivers in the lower reaches to dry up. The surface area of the Aral Sea, in the outer limits of Kazakhstan and Uzbekistan, decreased by 40 percent between 1960 and 1989; it is progressively becoming a salt-saturated desert. The construction of dams and reservoirs, either for irrigation or hydroelectric power, means the flooding of entire regions, interferes with the migration patterns of fish and can cause flooding downstream. Floods are also caused by logging, which chokes the rivers with earth and tree-trunks. Thanks to these problems, the control of rivers has become a frequent cause of conflict among different peoples. Another cause for concern is the dumping of untreated sewage and agricultural and industrial waste. The Danube, to give one example, is the victim of numerous ecological assaults, particularly by Germany where it has its source.

There is no lack of indicators leading us to believe that water is well on the way to becoming a scarce commodity. There can be no doubt that the occasional tensions that have already appeared are no more than early warnings of more serious conflicts to come. Fresh water supply poses one of the major challenges of the 21st century, unless an economical procedure is found for desalinating seawater in the next decade. Seas and oceans, however, will also become a major challenge, although to a lesser degree. The depletion of fishing grounds is already the source of great friction, as we have seen in the recent dispute between Spain and Morocco. In the future, the pollution of seas (not overlooking even the Mediterranean) may lead to conflict between countries along their shores.

The 1992 Earth Summit held in Rio de Janeiro, and the World

Conference on Climate Change held in Berlin in April 1995, confirmed that the market is not able to respond to threats to the environment
on a global scale. Furthermore, the Kyoto Protocol, signed in November 1997, and the World Summit on Sustainable Development, held
in Johannesburg from August 26 to September 4, 2002, showed that
the greenhouse effect could have catastrophic long-term consequences. This may not be certain, but if we wait for scientific verification
(or something which approximates it), it will be too late. By then, the
rise in sea level may have already caused irreparable damage and
the desertification of entire regions will be an accomplished fact.
Thanks to desertification, six million hectares of arable land disappear every year. Erosion, overexploitation and excessive pasturing
are reducing the availability of fertile land at an accelerated rate. As
a result, arid and semi-arid land is becoming desert; these lands can
no longer feed their inhabitants; flora and fauna are disappearing.

THE DEATH OF FORESTS

The main cause of the destruction of biodiversity and a great threat
to humanity is deforestation. In the last decade, 14 million square
kilometers of forest (30 times the surface area of Spain) have been
reduced to desert, while more than 30 million square kilometers currently face the same fate. This phenomenon could be stopped by
putting an end to indiscriminate logging, the cultivation of ecologically fragile terrains and excessive pasturing.

The basic threats to the ecological balance of the planet are the
industrial pollution of the developed nations and, at the regional
level, the poverty of the underdeveloped ones. This does not mean to
say we have reached the physical limits of production or the number
of inhabitants the Earth can take: it simply means that a series of
absurd political, economic and social conditions continues to allow
many human beings to die of hunger.

Each year, some 6,000 animal species are wiped off the face of the
Earth forever. The loss of biodiversity is occurring at a horrifying
pace: endangered today are 34 percent of fish species, 25 percent of

mammals, 25 percent of amphibians, 20 percent of reptiles, 11 percent of birds and 12.5 percent of all plant species. Meanwhile, forest fires send huge quantities of carbon dioxide into the atmosphere. Trees that may have been able to absorb the excess carbon dioxide are no longer there. To summarize: deforestation is one of the basic causes of the greenhouse effect.

Tropical forests are the most affected, losing between 1.5 percent and two percent of their surface area every year. In Indonesia, almost 80 percent of the rainforest of the island of Sumatra has disappeared since the 1970s. In Borneo, the rate of logging has increased by almost five times in the last 16 years. This devastation is largely due to the rapid growth of a population that uses wood as cooking fuel and works forestland for agriculture. Forest exploitation to satisfy demand in wealthy countries accounts for 20 percent of Third World logging. Deforestation is destroying a unique biological heritage: rainforests are home to 70 percent of the known species on the planet. There is no doubt that international trade is accelerating soil degradation and deforestation.

The notion of "sustainable development" is still making progress. The general idea is simple: development is sustainable if future generations can inherit an environment of at least the same quality that previous generations enjoyed. The question is whether the present logic of development, fundamentally based on the market, is really compatible with sustainability.

In this regard, the example of agriculture in Western Europe is instructive. In the name of productivism, many farmers have become industrial producers without any direct relationship with nature at all, as land is no longer needed for stockbreeding and agriculture. This rupturing of an ancestral bond has paved the way for all kinds of transgressions, particularly the treatment of animals as mere objects and the transformation of herbivores into carnivores, obligatory consumers of the remains of their own kind, be they healthy or contaminated. This perversion of the food chain in the name of deregulation and neoliberalism, exacerbated as it is by lax official health regulations, has led to the appearance of "mad cow disease," propagating yet another big scare across the old continent and beyond.

In all probability, two opposing dynamics will play pivotal roles in the fate of the planet over the next 10 years. First, the interests of the transnational companies, governed purely by financial criteria and using technoscience to the exclusive end of making profits. Second, a desire for ethics, responsibility and a more equitable kind of development, one that would not flinch from introducing restrictions to protect the environment. Without a doubt, this understanding is crucial for the future of humanity.

We must also consider the computer revolution, which has destructured contemporary society, disrupted the circulation of goods and favored both the digitalized economy and globalization itself. This has not yet forced all nations to merge into a single society, but it is pushing them into a single economic model by putting the whole planet online. It is creating a kind of neoliberal social link-up, constituted entirely of networks which divide humanity into monadic individuals in a hypertechnological universe.

The consequence: the logic of competition has been raised to the status of a natural imperative in society, when it is actually leading to the loss of the notions of "living together" and the "common good." Given that the benefits of productivity have been redistributed, favoring capital to the detriment of work, inequalities are deepening. In the United States, for example, one percent of the population owns 39 percent of the country's wealth. Solidarity is regarded as unaffordable and the edifice of the welfare state is being dismantled.[11]

With the brutality and speed of these changes, we have lost our way. Uncertainties are mounting, the world is becoming opaque and history shies away from any interpretation. Citizens feel trapped in the heart of the crises that arise, as in Antonio Gramsci's words, "when the old is not yet dead and the new not yet born." Or, as Alexis de Tocqueville said, "With the past no longer shedding light on the future, the mind advances in darkness."

NEOFASCISM

Out of this economic context, taking root in the social humus of fear and confusion, fascist-leaning parties are enjoying considerable popularity.

> Of the approximately 380 million people in the European Union — if, for a number of good reasons, we add Switzerland and Norway — 8.5 percent have voted for some variety of the far right. While it may not be very high, this figure conceals enormous variations at the national level. Thus, Switzerland, Italy and Austria have all registered about the same proportion of votes for the far right: about 25 percent. They are followed by Norway, France and Flanders with approximately 15 percent of the vote.[12]

In Denmark, the ultraright and xenophobic Danish People's Party gained 12 percent of the votes in the legislative elections of November 20, 2001, winning 22 seats in parliament.

In Holland, the Pim Fortuyn List won 34 percent of the votes in Rotterdam's municipal elections in March 2002. They went on to triumph in the legislative elections of May 15, which occurred nine days after the assassination of their leader.

In France, both the National Front (FN) of Jean-Marie Le Pen and the National Republican Movement of Bruno Mégret are proponents of a cult of blood and soil. They demand the restoration of the nation (in the ethnic sense of the term), the establishment of an authoritarian regime under the pretext of combating insecurity, drastic cuts to income tax, a return to economic protectionism, confining women to the home and expelling three million foreigners to free jobs for French males. According to one survey, "more than one in four French people are in favor of National Front ideas."[13]

Heirs of Petain and the collaboration, fed by the resentment of those who still yearn for French Algeria, these two parties (neither with any connection to the resistance) constantly flaunt racism, xenophobia and anti-Semitism, despite a few cosmetic touches. They incarnate the very antithesis of the values of the republic. In contrast to most of the other political groups, they are interclass parties where the bourgeoisie rub shoulders with the proletariat, owners of small businesses and the unemployed.[14] They have a presence in many problem neighborhoods, where they offer comfort and solidarity to the needy, their members demonstrating time and again the kind of zeal and abnegation that once characterized communists.[15] This commitment partly explains why their candidates win a considerable percentage of workers' votes in all elections, and why their influence continues to grow in some regions (Provence, the Alps, the Côte d'Azur and Alsace).

In December 2001, despite his party's discreet campaign in the run-up to the elections, the polls suggested that Jean-Marie Le Pen accounted for 11 percent of the intended vote in the presidential elections of May 2002, ranking him as the third candidate. As for Bruno Mégret, the opinion polls gave him between one percent and three percent of the intended vote. All in all, the forecast of the votes for the neofascists predicted a very impressive 15 percent (almost one in every six voters!), a figure equivalent to what they had achieved in the canton elections some months earlier.[16]

THE LE PEN EARTHQUAKE

The result, however, was even worse than what had been feared. More than 5.5 million French people (almost 20 percent of the voters!) voted for the far right on April 21, 2002, causing a political earthquake that rocked all of Europe. This was all the more shocking because Jean-Marie Le Pen won more votes than the prime minister and socialist candidate, Lionel Jospin, eliminating him from the presidential race.

This seismic upheaval should be considered in relation to the rise of national-populism in Italy, Austria, Switzerland, Portugal, Belgium, Denmark, Norway and Holland. The phenomenon essentially derives from the fact that our societies have undergone a series of traumatic and convulsive modifications over the last 10 years, yet without appreciable benefits to citizens, who have not understood the precise nature of these changes.

In other words, the end of the Cold War and the industrial era, the eruption of new technologies, neoliberal globalization, the hyperhegemony of the United States, European integration, the disappearance of national currencies, the elimination of borders, the loss of state sovereignty, the destruction of the welfare state, massive privatization and the arrival of vast numbers of immigrants with very different cultures, have forged an environment that is terrifying for many citizens who have witnessed the collapse of the world that was familiar to them. Many of them are afraid, haunted by new fears and new threats. Moreover, new terrors have been added to the existing fears: after September 11, 2001, the notion that Muslims, and therefore Maghreb immigrants, are terrorists and that Islam is a threat to European countries, has been gaining ground.

Once more, many voters consider that their leaders are not in control of the situation. Those in power face constant accusations from the media of being corrupt thieves and liars. As a result, political leaders seem incapable of responding to the challenge of the new world just as many have begun to think that the world is sinking. Those who think this way are usually the most vulnerable in our societies, the unemployed, workers, young people, the poor, the retired, the elderly, etc. They believe that a far right advocating authority, severity, tough measures, identity and patriotism might be the solution. The fact is that this national-populism merely proposes simplistic solutions for the complex problems of our societies, with the military or the police offered to solve political issues or problems of insecurity and delinquency. The people who vote for the far right are not militants of the far right, merely voters. Terrified by what is happening to them, these electors, in voting thus, also help terrorize the political system as a whole. What they drop into the urn is a bomb they hope will blow apart a political system that they feel neglects them.

In Italy today, as in other periods of contemporary history, these matters are somewhat more advanced. With Silvio Berlusconi at the helm, the renovated far right came to power for the first time in 1994. They won again in the elections of 2001, that time with an absolute majority. Many European observers commented mockingly on this phenomenon, attributing it to the local color of an Italy of tambourines and carnivals. They overlooked the fact that, as early as the 1920s, Italy served as the social and political laboratory for the creation of fascism, which later spread through Europe under slightly different forms such as Nazism or the Falangist movement, bringing about the tragedy of World War II.

Following the Le Pen scare in France and the rise of the extreme xenophobic right in Holland, many commentators have realized that Italy has once again been the precursor of a political phenomenon spreading throughout Europe. It already affects Norway, Denmark, Austria, Switzerland, Belgium, Ireland, Portugal and France. Sometimes, because of intellectual laziness, these movements have been lumped together under the heading of "fascism." This is an error.

The new hard-line right-wing parties are actually more national-populist by nature: they have abandoned the cult of the state, a key characteristic of traditional fascism; they accept the democratic game; they are more regionalist than nationalist, for example, Umberto Bossi's Northern League, or the Vlaams Block in Flanders; they are ultraliberal in matters concerning the economy while remaining fiercely protectionist in favor of suppressing direct taxes. They also support the FN line with regard to foreigners. In this respect, while some parties openly advocate the expulsion of foreigners, as Le Pen's National Front does, others only demand that no more illegal immigrants should be allowed in. Such parties favor the integration of those foreigners who are already installed in the country, although they oppose family reunification (bringing other family members (husbands, wives or children) who have remained in the country of origin).

All of these movements fervently support a restoration of authority. They call for tougher measures against delinquency and swift legal action that will mete out punishment without blinking an eye.

All are opposed to multiculturalism, or the coexistence of different foreign cultures within the same society. They are especially appalled by the presence of Islam and all that it entails: the construction of mosques, religious festivities, traditional clothing, etc.

Their voters come from two very different social categories: the very poor, who are the most affected by globalization, and the very rich, who fear social democratic programs that redistribute wealth and increase taxes. They all have very traditional, homogenous conceptions of their respective societies and fear any modification of the religious and ethnic composition of their countries. For them, this would constitute a crime of impurity. Immigrants represent the height of all evil and all fears to those of the new right: job-stealing, delinquency, sexual rivalry, drugs, religious threat and ethnic degeneration.

Even those who had always voted for the left have begun to vote for these neofascist parties, and former militants of traditional right-wing parties do not hesitate to join them. A number of studies have established that only one percent of the FN party officials come from the far right, in comparison with 40 percent from the "Gaullist movements."[17] Some political personalities openly seek the support of neofascists, arguing that the socialist parties have never had scruples about allying themselves with communists. This is a lamentable effect of the thesis of *The Black Book of Communism*.[18] Michel Poniatowski has gone so far as to state, "It is more immoral to accept the votes of communists, who have killed millions of people in Europe, than the votes of the National Front."[19]

In the Germany of the early 1930s, this kind of thinking led the traditional right to choose as their ally the National-Socialist (Nazi) Party, which had presented itself in its most seductive guises.[20] There is no need to describe here what happened to the right-wing parties. Or what happened to democracy...

In Italy, Silvio Berlusconi has not hesitated to ally himself with the profascist National Alliance Party and the xenophobic Northern League in order to win the legislative elections on two occasions, in

1994 and 2001. Formerly, he was the protégé of the Socialist Party and friend of its one-time leader, Bettino Craxi.

Whatever the electoral survey, the signs are that abstention is on the rise, as are blank votes and nonappearance on electoral rolls. In France, one out of every three people under the age of 25 did not figure on the rolls on the eve of the May 2002 presidential elections. The figure for party affiliations is less than two percent of voters and only eight percent of wage earners belong to a union. These figures are the lowest in the western world.

THE STAGNATION OF THE LEFT

The French Communist Party no longer has political identity on the left, and has even lost a good part of its sociological identity. As for socialist parties, hardly any of their officials come from the working class.

Socialism, one of the great unifying myths of humanity, has similarly been betrayed by European social democratic leaders. The March 12, 1999, resignation of Oskar Lafontaine, German minister for the economy, spectacularly revealed the stagnation of the social democratic movement and its inability to offer any proposal that would represent an alternative to neoliberal hegemony. Even Keynesianism, which enabled President Franklin Delano Roosevelt to pull the United States out of the crisis of the 1930s, would be too left wing in social democratic eyes today. Oskar Lafontaine was accused by his own social democratic comrades of having committed five sacrileges: advocating a policy of European resurgence; defending a more equitable tax system; criticizing the European Central Bank; calling for reforms to the international monetary system; and on one occasion asking the Bundesbank to lower its interest rates to make loans more accessible, an attempt to encourage consumption and combat unemployment.

Another example of the intellectual sell-out of social democracy is the Kosovo War, which began on March 23, 1999. We should not forget that it was Javier Solana, then secretary general of NATO, who announced the decision to end negotiations with the Belgrade regime and start bombing Serbia. Javier Solana, as one of the founders of the Spanish Socialist Workers' Party, could count on the inestimable support of Gerhard Schröder, Lionel Jospin, Massimo d'Alema and Tony Blair in that war, the heads of state of Germany, France, Italy and the United Kingdom respectively: all were eminent members of the European social democratic movement. In order to break the impasse of the Rambouillet peace negotiations, they accepted the military option proposed by Washington as the "only solution." None of them were ignorant of the fact that resorting to the bombing of Serbia would mean the deaths of numerous innocent civilians and the destruction of an entire country. Nor would it avoid an escalation of the conflict to the Balkans, as the Macedonia War demonstrated in 2001.

These social democratic leaders were the heirs of Jean Jaurès and come from a long tradition of respecting international law: how could they cave in so readily to pressure from Washington, and embark upon the military adventure of Kosovo without a shred of international legitimacy? Not one of the UN resolutions referring to this region explicitly authorized the use of force. The Security Council, the world's supreme body for dealing with conflicts, was not consulted before the bombing started and therefore was never given the chance to approve the use of arms against Serbia.

Finally, it did not occur to even one of the social democratic leaders to explain the situation to their respective parliaments before the hostilities began, and still less to ask them for authorization to commit the nations' armed forces to this conflict.

How is it not possible to see in these examples still more signs of the ideological collapse of social democracy and its conversion to neoliberalism? It has lost its bearings and, in the absence of any theoretical anchor (unless we use the term "theory" to describe those catalogs of renunciation and recantation like *The Global Third Way Debate* by Anthony Giddens,[21] adviser to Tony Blair, and *The Politics of the New Center* by Bodo Hombach,[22] source of inspiration to Gerhard

Schröder) social democracy has been left adrift due to its obsession with urgency and immediacy.

THE MODERN RIGHT

For social democracy, which governs in its own right in several major European nations, politics is economy, economy is finance, and finance is markets. Accordingly, political efforts are geared toward privatization, dismantling the public sector and macrobusiness takeovers and mergers. Despite major social laws occasionally being passed,[23] the fact remains that social democracy has accepted the conversion to social neoliberalism. By abandoning the aims of full employment and the eradication of poverty, social democracy has abandoned any pretense of responding to the needs of the 18 million unemployed and 50 million poor who live in the European Union.

Social democracy won the intellectual battle after the fall of the Berlin Wall in 1989. The conservative parties were the losers and they prepared themselves to leave history behind just as the aristocracy had to do after 1789, and radicalism after 1945. In the political spectrum today, however, the left is yet to be reinvented. The defense of conformity and conservatism has become the task of social democracy, making it today's right.[24] In its theoretical bankruptcy and opportunism, it has taken on the historical mission of acclimatizing the world to neoliberalism. In the name of "realism," it no longer wants to change. Especially nothing related to the social order.

For many, the neoliberal thesis that the West is now mature enough to exist in absolute freedom is as utopian, and as dogmatic, as the revolutionary ambition of absolute egalitarianism. People wonder how to think of the future, expressing the need for a new rationalization of the world, another utopia. They are awaiting some kind of political prophecy, a sensible plan for the future, the promise of a reconciled society in total harmony with itself.

Now that socialist dreams have been destructured by neoliberal barbarism, is there any space left for a new utopia? It seems barely possible, given the now-generalized suspicion of large-scale political projects. At the same time, we are in the midst of a grave crisis of political representation, an enormous discrediting of the technocratic elites and intellectuals, and an unbreachable rift between the mass media and its public.

There are many citizens who would like to be able to add a pinch of humanity to the work of neoliberalism. They seek a model of responsible involvement and feel the need for collective action. They would like to see the faces of those who are politically responsible; they want them to be clearly defined, flesh-and-blood people on to whom they can unload their reproaches, concerns, worries and sense of disorientation. The reality, however, is that power has become something abstract, invisible, distant and impersonal. They would like to continue to believe that politics has the answers to everything, when the reality is that they want clear, simple solutions to the complex problems of society.

All in all, we all feel the need to construct a wall against the neoliberal tide: a global counterproject, a counterideology, or a conceptual edifice that is capable of opposing the dominant model we have today. Setting up such a counterproject is far from easy, as we would practically be starting out from a *tabula rasa*. Earlier progressive utopias frequently fell into the trap of authoritarianism, oppression, the suppression of freedoms and the manipulation of consciousness.

Once again there is a tangible need for dreamers who think and thinkers who dream. We need to move beyond mere jargon and on to an assessment of society that can enable the timely replacement of neoliberal ideology with a whole new conceptual structure.

CITIZENS' RESPONSES

Fostering fragmentation and partition, neoliberal ideology creates a selfish society. It is therefore necessary to reintroduce collective values that hold the seeds of the future.[25] At present, collective action is channeled through associations and NGOs as much as through political parties and unions. In recent years, Europe has seen a proliferation of associations and NGOs, from ATTAC to Right to Housing

(DAL), from Act Together Against Unemployment (AC!) to the AIDS Coalition to Unleash Power (Act Up), along with local branches of big international NGOs such as Greenpeace, Amnesty International, Medicus Mundi, Transparency and Global Media Watch.

Parties have, *inter alia*, two characteristics that continue to make them unviable: they are generalist (claiming they can solve all of society's problems) and local (their radius of action ends with the country's borders). Associations and NGOs, on the contrary, have symmetrically opposite attributes: they are thematic (tackling one social problem at a time: the power of finance, unemployment, housing, environment, etc.) and transnational (their areas of activity cover the entire planet).[26]

Over the last decade, the two forms of commitment (global commitment and immediate commitment to a specific cause) have turned their backs on each other on more than one occasion. At present, however, some movement toward convergence is discernible and a consolidation of this trend is indispensable. This is one of the problems to be resolved if politics is to be restored to its true role. Even if these associations appear to be a testimony to the richness of civil society and a palliative to the deficiencies of unionism and the parties, many are no more than simple pressure groups lacking the power of political representation. Sooner or later, political action takes over. It is therefore of crucial importance that the link between these associations and political parties is forged now.

Citizens' associations based on a radical conviction of democracy are acting on the belief that another world is possible. There is no doubt that they are the embryonic renaissance of political action in Europe. In all probability, their members believe in positive utopias as they were heralded in the words of Victor Hugo ("Utopia is the truth of tomorrow") and Lamartine ("Utopias are nothing but premature truths"). Each year since 2001, the People's Assembly has been held at the World Social Forum (WSF) of Porto Alegre. Five billion of the world's six billion inhabitants are represented. The Porto Alegre

Forum represents humanity. Meeting at the end of January each year, for the first time in history, is humanity itself.[27]

It calls to reestablish the United Nations at the heart of international law, an institution capable of deciding, acting and imposing a project of permanent peace; it supports the establishment of international courts of justice to deal with crimes against humanity, democracy and the common good; it condemns the manipulation of the media; it demands an end to discrimination against women, the establishment of new ecological rights and the principle of sustainable development, the abolition of tax havens, the stimulation of an economy of solidarity etc.

"Dare to go down paths no one has walked, dare to think ideas no one has thought," could be read on the walls of the Paris Odeón Theater in May 1968. If we truly wish to establish ethical principles for the 21st century, the present situation calls for just such daring.

SEPTEMBER 11, 2001
WORLD WAR AGAINST TERRORISM

It was September 11. Deflected from their programmed route by pilots who would stop at nothing, the planes hurtled toward the heart of the big city. Their mission: to bring down the symbol of a detested political system. It all happened very fast: explosions, the destruction of buildings, the infernal din of collapsing facades, the terror of the survivors fleeing, covered in dust... and the mass media broadcasting the tragedy live to air.

New York, 2001? No, Santiago de Chile, September 11, 1973. With the United States as its accomplice, the Chilean Air Force was systematically bombing the presidential palace, in a coup d'état led by General Pinochet against the socialist president, Salvador Allende. Dozens were killed at the start of a reign of terror that was to last 17 years.

Our legitimate compassion aside for the victims of the execrable attacks in New York on September 11, 2001, how can we dispute the fact that the United States is no more innocent than any other country? Has it not engaged in violent, illegal and clandestine political acts in Latin America, Africa, the Middle East and Asia, with a tragic toll of deaths, "disappearances," torture victims, prisoners and exiles?

Neither the attitude of western leaders and the mass media, nor their pro-U.S. fervor in the wake of the criminal attacks of September 11, should conceal the cruel reality from us. Throughout the world, and especially in underdeveloped countries, the public sentiment most frequently voiced following the tragedy was, "What happened to them is very sad, but they had it coming."

Paradoxically, in many regions of the planet, these horrific attacks have inspired not waves of sympathy for the United States, but the contrary. This was so much the case that George W. Bush declared he was shocked that there was such ignorance about the United States and that its people were so hated. Like the majority of U.S. citizens, he could not believe this hatred because he knew that the United States was "good."

THE BLACK BOOK OF THE COLD WAR

In order to understand the hostile reactions toward the United States, it would not be excessive to recall that, during the "Cold War" (1948–89), the United States launched a long "crusade" against communism. In some cases, this crusade reached the proportions of a war of extermination: thousands of communists eliminated in Iran, 200,000 members of the left-wing opposition exterminated in Guatemala, more than half a million communists massacred in Indonesia... The most abominable pages of the black book of U.S. imperialism were written during those years, and were equally blotted with the horrors of the Vietnam War (1962–75).

Even then, it was "Good against Evil." According to Washington, however, supporting certain terrorists at that time was not necessarily immoral. Through its Central Intelligence Agency (CIA), the United States organized attacks in public places, the disappearance of opponents, the hijackings of aircraft, acts of sabotage and killings. In Cuba, it was against the regime of Fidel Castro; in Nicaragua, against the Sandinistas; in Afghanistan, against the Russians. In Afghanistan, with the support of two very undemocratic states (Saudi Arabia and Pakistan), the United States sponsored the creation of Islamic brigades in the 1970s. They were recruited from around the Muslim Arab world and composed of what were then known as "freedom fighters." Fighters for freedom! Now a well-known fact, these were the circumstances in which the CIA recruited and trained the now-famous Osama Bin Laden.

Since 1991, the United States alone has occupied the position of the single hyperpower, effectively elbowing aside the United Nations. In compensation, it promised to usher in a more just "international order." In the name of this project, the United States led and won the 1991 Gulf War against Iraq. It continued to act with a scandalous bias toward Israel and against the rights of the Palestinians.[1] As if this were not enough, it turned a deaf ear to international protests and maintained an implacable embargo against Iraq, causing the deaths of thousands of innocent people and leaving the regime intact. This "New World Order" did not seem any more just in the eyes of the millions of inhabitants of the developing countries. All of this outraged the feelings of the Arab and Muslim worlds, encouraging the creation of a breeding ground for radical, anti-U.S. Islam.

Like a latter-day doctor Frankenstein, on September 11, 2001, the United States saw its old creation — Osama Bin Laden — rise up against it with demented violence. It decided to combat this with the support of the very two states — Saudi Arabia and Pakistan — that have most contributed to the spread of radical Islamic networks all over the world in the last 30 years, never flinching from terrorist methods when they were considered opportune.

THE THREAT OF PAKISTAN

If there is one country with a tragic political tradition, it is Pakistan. Not a single head of state of this country of 140 million inhabitants has ever relinquished power voluntarily. Born in 1947 with the British Empire's partition of India, when millions of Muslims and Hindus fled in apocalyptic conditions from the regions where they were minorities, the "Land of the Pure" was the world's first state to be created artificially on the basis of a religion: Islam.

Time has revealed the incapacity of this religious cement to hold together a nation. The 1971 secession of East Pakistan, which then became Bangladesh, demonstrated that ethnic criteria could be more powerful than religious ones. The other ingredient of cohesion, hatred of India, also revealed its limitations in the three wars fought between the two countries, in 1947, 1965 and 1971, each war ending in Pakistan's defeat.

Before the tensions of spring 2002, the last major confrontation between India and Pakistan had occurred in July 1999, over control of the Kargil Heights in Kashmir. Both Islamabad and New Delhi consider that Kashmir is a vital issue for the identity of each nation. This region, with a Muslim majority, has been divided by an armistice line since 1948. The southern part of Kashmir is administered by India, which faces determined resistance led by Islamic separatist organizations (clandestinely supported by Osama Bin Laden's al-Qaida network). The organizations Lashkar-e-Taïba and Jaish-e-Mohammad, the secret services of Pakistan, have no qualms about resorting to the most extreme forms of violence or perpetrating attacks with a great deal of bloodshed. They claimed responsibility for the assault on the Indian Parliament of December 13, 2001, in which 14 people died, once again pushing the two countries to the brink of war.

Further Islamic attacks in May and June 2002 occasioned a new and brutal outbreak of war fever. All along the Kashmir border, both nations mobilized more than a million soldiers ready for all-out war. The combined populations of India and Pakistan amount to 1.2 billion people, or a fifth of the world's population. The whole planet was terrified by the prospect of this clash, as it was the first time in history that two countries with nuclear capacity could have gone to war. Any use of atomic weaponry by either side would have caused some 12 million deaths in the days succeeding the attack. The injured would have taken up all the hospital beds of every country from Japan to Egypt. The consequences in terms of a generalized increase in radioactivity would have been dire for all humanity. This tragic war would also have launched millions of Indian and Pakistani emigrants, fleeing the horrors of nuclear war, toward neighboring states and the rich countries. The domino effect would have been incredible.

There is little doubt that Pakistan's military defeat in the summer of 1990, followed by the humiliating withdrawal of its invading forces, in accordance with the demands of Islamabad's old ally Washington, brought about the overthrow of Nawaz Sharif by General Pervez Musharraf on October 12, 1999. It was the first time since the end of the Cold War that a military coup had occurred in such an important country and, more serious still, in a country possessing nuclear weapons. The only Islamic country with the atomic bomb, a state that is falling apart and led by military men, Pakistan also has long-range nuclear missiles with a reach of 1,500 kilometers.

To make matters worse, this is a nuclear power located in an extremely dangerous part of the world. The country faces the hostility of two of its neighbors, India and Iran, and the increasing distrust of its former ally, China. Prior to the attacks of September 11, 2001, and the U.S. response, Pakistan had tolerated the extremist activism of a friendly state, the quasi-protectorate of Afghanistan. Afghanistan took in and sheltered Islamic networks — like Bin Laden's al-Qaida — that were directly or indirectly fostered by Saudi Arabia (another ally of Islamabad). The influence of these terrorist networks extended as far as the formerly Russian territories of Central Asia (Uzbekistan, Tajikistan, Turkmenistan) and the north of the Caucasus region (Dagestan and Chechnya, which formed part of the Russian Federation).

On the edge of bankruptcy, Pakistan is one of the main platforms of Islamic fundamentalism. In the domestic sphere, the issue is a powder keg. The nation is divided by religious dissent, with Sunnis opposed to Shi'ites (20 percent of the population), ethnic clashes between Pathans, Baluchis, Sindhis and Punjabis, and social in-

equality: 40 percent of the population lives below the poverty line
and some 20 million children work as slaves. Moreover, this is one
of the most corrupt countries in the world. According to the United
Nations, it has a black market economy that surpasses the legal
economy in total value. Yet none of this has prevented the Bush
Administration from abandoning all scruples and making Pakistan
its main ally in South Asia.

AN ADVERSARY AT LAST!

Cold War veterans, the men and women around George W. Bush
cannot complain about the turn of events following September 11.
One can even imagine them rubbing their hands with glee. Miracu-
lously, the attacks have restored the fundamental strategic element
that the collapse of the Soviet Union in 1991 had deprived them of
for over a decade: an adversary. At last!

Labeled "international terrorism," the chosen adversary is radical
Islamism. This justified all the excessive, authoritarian measures,
including a modern version of McCarthyism that would soon target
not only terrorist organizations, but all those who oppose U.S. hegemony, including opponents of global neoliberalization.

Embarking upon the first armed conflict of the 21st century, the
United States immediately set about achieving a number of military
goals. The first aim was announced on the day after September 11: to
dismantle the al-Qaida network and to capture "dead or alive"
Osama Bin Laden, responsible for crimes — the deaths of some 3,000
people — that cannot be justified under any circumstances.

This aim, while simple to formulate, was not so easy to accom-
plish, although the evident discrepancy in power between the two
sides seemed vast. If the truth be told, the military situation could
not have been more unusual: it was the first time an empire had declared war, not against a state, but against an individual.

With its overwhelming military capacity, Washington launched
a full-scale attack and could do nothing less than win. Yet, at the
beginning, there were many who were not so sure of a victory for the

United States. History is replete with examples of great powers that were unable to finish off weaker adversaries. In fact, military history teaches that, in asymmetrical combat, the side with the greatest capacity cannot always complete the smallest task. As historian Eric Hobsbawm points out, "In almost 30 years, the British have been unable to eliminate an army like the IRA, which, though it has of course not won, it has not been vanquished either."[2]

Like most armies, that of the United States is organized to fight other states, not to confront an "invisible enemy." In this new century, however, wars between states are well on the way to becoming an anachronism. The crushing victory of the Gulf War is not a good reference point. It may even be deceptive as an example. "Our 1991 offense in the Gulf was victorious," says Anthony Zinni, former U.S. marines general, "because we were lucky enough to be dealing with the only bad guy in the world stupid enough to take on the United States in one-to-one combat."[3] The same might be said of Slobodan Milosevic with regard to the Kosovo War in 1999.

This new type of conflict, where the strong side engages with the weak or crazy side, is much easier to begin than to end. The use of ultramodern military means, as massive as they might be, does not necessarily guarantee that the goals will be accomplished. It is sufficient to recall the failures of the United States in Vietnam in 1975 and Somalia in 1994. In attacking Afghanistan (with the convincing pretext that the Taliban regime in this country was protecting Bin Laden), the U.S. Government was perfectly aware that it was initiating the simplest phase of the conflict, confident it would be over in a matter of weeks with a minimal number of U.S. casualties. Nonetheless, victory over one of the most detested regimes on Earth did not assure the achievement of the prime objective of the war: the capture of Bin Laden.

The second U.S. aim seems altogether too ambitious: to put an end to "international terrorism." First, the term "terrorism" is imprecise. It has been indiscriminately used over the last two centuries to designate all those who, rightly or wrongly, resort to violence to change the political order. Experience shows that, in some cases, this violence was necessary. "*Sic semper tirannis,*" exclaimed Brutus on stabbing Julius Caesar, who had overthrown the Republic. In 1792, French revolutionary Gracchus Babeuf stated, "All means used to struggle against tyrants are legitimate."

Many former "terrorists" have eventually become respectable statespeople. For example, without mentioning all the French leaders who came out of the Resistance, and who had been described as "terrorists" by the German occupation authorities, we can cite Menahem Begin, the former head of Irgun who became prime minister of Israel; Abdelaziz Buteflika, once leader of the Algerian National Liberation Front and subsequently president of Algeria; and Nelson Mandela, the African National Congress (ANC) head who became president of South Africa and a Nobel Peace Prize laureate.

The present-day "world war against terrorism" and its accompanying propaganda may give the impression that the only form of terrorism is Islamic. Evidently this is not the case. Even as this new "world war" is unfolding, a number of "terrorist" organizations are still active in almost every corner of the non-Islamic world: ETA in Spain, the FARC and the paramilitaries in Colombia, the Tamil Tigers in Sri Lanka and, until very recently, the IRA and the Unionists in Northern Ireland, to name but a few. Depending on the circumstances, almost every political family has defended terrorism as a principle of action. The first theoretician to propose a doctrine of terrorism was Germany's Karl Heinzen in his 1848 essay *Der Mord* (Murder), where he stated that all means, including suicide attacks, are valid if they speed up the advent of... democracy! As a radical democrat, Heinzen wrote the following:

> If, to destroy the party of the barbarians, it is necessary to blow up half a continent and cause a bloodbath, don't have any qualms of conscience. Anyone who is not disposed to willingly offer up his life for the satisfaction of exterminating a million barbarians is not a true republican.[4]

The absurdity of this example shows that not even the best of ends can justify all the means. Citizens would do well to fear the worst in any republic — lay or religious — that is built on a bloodbath. Nowadays, it is generally accepted that resorting to terrorist violence in a context of real political democracy (like Northern Ireland, the Basque region of Spain, or Corsica) is inadmissible.

It is equally wise to fear that the universal hunt for "terrorists" announced by Washington as the final objective of this "war without end," could lend itself to dangerous abuse and attacks against basic freedoms. If we accept that the tragic events of September 11, 2001, have ushered in a new period of history, we can at least wonder what cycle was closed by this occurrence and what its consequences might be.

The period that has just ended began on November 9, 1989, with the fall of the Berlin Wall, and was confirmed with the disappearance of the Soviet Union on December 25, 1991. Constantly celebrated, the basic characteristics of this stage — which also saw the takeoff of neoliberal globalization — have been an exaltation of the democratic system, the quintessence of democracy, and the glorification of human rights. Both in internal affairs and foreign policy, this modern trinity has been the constantly evoked categorical imperative. While it did not lack ambiguities (is it really possible to reconcile neoliberal globalization and democracy?), it was supported by citizens who saw it as the victory of the rule of law over barbarism.

In this respect, September 11, 2001, marks a clear turning point. In the name of a "just war" against terrorism, all of these generous ideas seem to have been suddenly forgotten. For a start, just before attacking Afghanistan, Washington did not hesitate to set up alliances with leaders who today are considered undesirable: the Pakistan coup-maker, General Pervez Musharraf, and the dictator of Uzbekistan, Islam Karimov. The cries of the legitimate Pakistani president, Nawaz Sharif, and of the defenders of freedom in Uzbekistan, did not filter through the dungeon walls. Ethical values once described as "fundamental" slipped noiselessly from the political scene, while, in legal terms, democratic states went into regression.

This has been confirmed by the avalanche of freedom-killing measures adopted by the U.S. Government, which introduced extraordinary legal measures the day after the attacks. The attorney general, John Ashcroft, pushed through an antiterrorist bill by the name of The Patriot Act. It permitted the authorities to detain suspicious foreigners almost indefinitely, to deport them, lock them in isolation cells, monitor their mail, telephone conversations and internet communications and to search their homes without a warrant.

In the application of this law, no less than 1,200 foreigners were secretly detained.[5] Over 600 of them remained in prison at the end of December 2001, many of them without ever appearing before a judge or being offered legal assistance. The U.S. Government also declared its intention of interrogating 5,000 men aged between 16 and 45 years who had entered the country on tourist visas. They were considered suspects for the simple fact of having come from the Middle East.[6]

In May 2002, the U.S. Government ceded unlimited powers to the Federal Bureau of Investigation (FBI): they could now spy on U.S. citizens, intrude in their gatherings (even those held in churches, synagogues or mosques), infiltrate their political meetings and snoop on their e-mails and chatroom conversations under the pretext of looking for terrorists. The revamped FBI thus became a kind of domestic CIA, an internal security and espionage agency with unlimited powers to knock on the door of any person they considered suspicious, even if nothing and no one could link him or her with any terrorist plot.[7]

Along the same lines was President Bush's announcement of the most far-reaching reforms to the security system since 1947, the year President Harry Truman created the Pentagon, the CIA and the National Security Council. This followed the revelations of the errors committed by the FBI and the CIA before September 11 that had meant the failure to prevent the tragic attacks. On June 6, 2002, George W. Bush is quoted as saying:

We know that thousands of terrorists are conspiring to attack us and this tremendous realization has obliged us to act differently. The United States, as leader of the civilized world, must continue and be more effective in its titanic fight against terrorism.[8]

The president therefore decided to create a superministry against terrorism, a new department that would regroup 22 agencies and services, with 170,000 state employees and a budget of more than €37 billion.

Although the ordinary courts of the United States are perfectly competent to try foreigners accused of terrorism,[9] by November 13, 2001, President George W. Bush had already created military tribunals with special procedures. The secret trials could now take place on warships and in military bases;[10] sentences would be pronounced by a commission formed by army officers; unanimity would not be necessary for condemning an accused to death; there would be no appeal on the verdict; conversations between the accused and their lawyer could be tapped; the legal procedure would take place behind closed doors and no details of the trial would be made public for decades.

RESORTING TO TORTURE?

FBI officials have gone so far as to propose that certain suspects be extradited to friendly countries with dictatorial regimes, so the local police can interrogate them using "violent, expeditious and effective" methods. Resorting to violence and torture in this way has been openly called for in the columns of leading magazines.[11] Republican commentator Tucker Carlson was quite explicit on CNN, stating that "torture is not good but terrorism is worse." He reasoned that, "in certain circumstances, torture is the lesser evil." In the *Chicago Tribune*, Steve Chapman reminded his readers that a democratic state like Israel does not flinch from applying torture, or "moderate physical pressure," to 85 percent of its Palestinian prisoners.[12]

On Sunday, January 20, 2002, the top-rated CBS program "60 Minutes," was devoted to the issue of whether torturing Taliban detainees was justified or not. It offered the testimony of the French general, Paul Aussaresses, who admitted having used torture against patriots in the Algerian War (1954–62). He was condemned by the legal system of his own country for "complicity with and apologizing for war crimes." CBS justified the use of this testimony, arguing that General Aussaresses was defending a method (torture) for avoiding the deaths of innocent people at the hands of terrorists.

After revoking a 1974 decision which prohibited the CIA from assassinating foreign leaders, President Bush gave the agency *carte blanche* to carry out any secret operations it deemed necessary to achieve the physical elimination of al-Qaida. Ignoring the Geneva Conventions, the war in Afghanistan was waged in the same spirit: execute al-Qaida members even if they surrender. U.S. Secretary of Defense Donald Rumsfeld, was inflexible, rejecting any possibility of a negotiated solution and surrender, declaring, "We do not want any al-Qaida terrorist to escape. We want to prevent the setting up of the network in any other part of the world. We'll clean out the Tora Bora caves one by one if necessary." He went on to make a clear call for the assassination of all Arab and non-Afghan prisoners who were fighting for the Taliban.[13] More than 400 Taliban combatants were exterminated in the uprising at the Qalae-Jhangi fortress and an undoubtedly higher number after the taking of Tora Bora.

This all suggests that Washington simply did not want any member of the terrorist sect of al-Qaida to survive, not even when they surrendered and became prisoners. On several occasions, for example in Kandahar and Tora Bora, U.S. officers on the ground were inflexible in their refusal to accept the pacts and surrender agreements established between al-Qaida members and allied anti-Taliban forces. The combat had to continue until all survivors had been liquidated. "All the al-Qaida fighters must be killed and killed now! Laying down their arms will not be accepted," the CIA ordered the alliance combatants on the Tora Bora front.

Another crime was committed with the indiscriminate use of cluster bombs, prohibited under the terms of the Ottawa Convention.

Highly controversial, these bombs are like babushka dolls, with smaller bombs inside them. Every B-52 drops some 30 big bombs (CBU-87), each of which scatters more than 200 small bombs (LU-97), and each of these in turn frees 300 yellow grenades about the size of a beer can. Thus, every cluster bomb scatters more than 60,000 bombs and a single B-52 drops more than 1.8 million explosive devices at a time! Let us remember that in some areas these planes were bombing for weeks at a time without letup.

A CBU-87 bomb destroys everything, people and materials, in an area equivalent to a dozen football fields. About 10 percent of the small yellow bombs do not explode when they hit the ground. Hidden by sand or shrubs, they therefore function as antipersonnel or antivehicle mines and go on exacting their toll among innocent rural dwellers long after they have been dropped.

To ensure that U.S. military personnel are not brought to trial for operations carried out abroad, Washington refuses to ratify the agreement that would establish the International Criminal Court (ICC). To this effect, the Senate has approved, on first reading, the American Service Members Protection Act (ASPA), which permits the United States to take extreme measures — even the invasion of a country — to bring home any U.S. citizen in danger of being called before the ICC. Other countries such as the United Kingdom, Germany, Italy, Spain and France have similarly used the pretext of the "world war against terrorism" to toughen their repressive legislation.

Defenders of civil rights have more than enough reasons for being disturbed. The general tendency that our societies had toward an ever-greater respect for the individual and his or her freedoms has been brutally cut short. Everything indicates that the present drift is toward the increasingly policed state. In its annual report on the state of human rights around the world, presented on May 28, 2002, Amnesty International confirms this trend. They denounced the fact that several governments have taken advantage of September 11 and the wave of indignation that followed it to climb on to the "anti-terrorism" bandwagon, using the cruel event to "increase repression, undermine the protection of human rights and repress political dissidence."[14]

A RADICAL GEOPOLITICAL CHANGE

We are therefore witnessing a geopolitical metamorphosis that will irremediably affect our lives. It all began on that fateful day, Tuesday, September 11, 2001, with the discovery of a new weapon. A commercial aircraft full of fuel, was transformed into a missile of destruction and an immense firebomb. Previously unknown, the monstrous new weapon exploded in several places in a very short time, taking the United States by surprise. The violence of the impact was so great that it effectively shook the whole world.

What changed, for a start, was the very perception of terrorism. The term "hyperterrorism"[15] was immediately coined to underline the fact that terrorism would never be the same again. An unthinkable, inconceivable limit had now been exceeded. The disproportion of the aggression turned it into an unprecedented event, so unprecedented that nobody knew what to call it. Outrage? Attack? Act of war? The limits of extreme violence seem to have been extended. There is no going back. We all know that the crimes of September 11 — the premiere — will recur.[16] It may be somewhere else, in other circumstances, but it will happen again. The history of conflicts shows that a new weapon will always be used, however horrible its effects. This is confirmed by the continued use of nerve gas after 1918, or the destruction of cities in bombing raids after Guernica in 1937. In short, this is the fear perpetuated, 50 years after Hiroshima, by the nuclear threat.

Apart from its astonishing cruelty, the aggression of September 11 reveals a high level of complexity in its authors. They wanted to hit their victims hard, hit them where it hurts most and, above all, hit at their consciousness. They tried to achieve at least three effects: enormous material damage, symbolic impact and huge media uproar.

The outcome is all too well known: about 3,000 human lives lost, the destruction of the two towers of the World Trade Center and one wing of the Pentagon. If a fourth plane had not crashed in Pennsylvania, the White House would probably have been destroyed too. Yet it is clear that this damage was not the main aim, otherwise the planes would have targeted dams, reservoirs, or nuclear power stations, to provoke apocalyptic catastrophes and tens of thousands of deaths.[17]

The second aim was to make an impression on the collective imagination, by discrediting, offending and humiliating the basic symbols of the grandeur of the United States, the outward signs of its imperial hegemony in the economic (the World Trade Center), military (Pentagon) and political (White House) spheres.

The third objective, though less evident than the other two, was in the realm of the mass media. In a kind of television coup d'état, Osama Bin Laden (presumably the brains behind the attack), aimed to take over the screens. Like some kind of diabolical television producer, he imposed on them the images of his destructive work. Seriously damaging the U.S. Administration,[18] he took control of all the television screens in the United States and beyond. This enabled him to give unmistakable proof of the vulnerability of the number one hyperpower; to flaunt his own evil power within the walls of U.S. homes; and to personally stage his choreographed crime.

MEDIA MESSIANISM

The photograph of Osama Bin Laden himself was a display of narcissism which complemented the other dominant images of this crisis. With an Afghan cave as the backdrop, this was the self-portrait of a man with a strange sweetness in his gaze. Overnight, this image transformed Bin Laden, practically unknown on the eve of September 11, into the most famous person in the world.[19]

Ever since technology made it possible to send direct images around the planet, the world has been ripe for the emergence of "media messianism." The case of Diana (princess of Wales), particularly demonstrated that the mass media, now much greater in size, is also more unified and homogenized than ever before. Sooner or later, this state of affairs would have to be turned to the advantage of some kind of electronic prophet.[20]

Osama Bin Laden is the first. The aggression of September 11 gave him access to every screen in the world and enabled him to convey his message on a planetary scale. This genius of evil, for many a latter-day Dr. Marbuse, was simultaneously able to appear in the eyes of millions of people, especially in the Arab Muslim world, as a hero and, even more than a hero, as a messiah: he who is chosen and sent by God to deliver humanity from evil.

With his messianic aim, paradoxical as it may seem, he did not hesitate to invent a new kind of terrorism. It is obvious that, from now on, we will have to deal with terror on a worldwide scale, in its organization, scope and goals. It does not have very precise claims. It does not call for the independence of some territory or for specific political concessions, or the installation of a particular type of regime. This new form of terror functions as a form of punishment or warning against the "general behavior" (without further detail) of the United States and, more inclusively, of the entire western world.

Both President George W. Bush — who spoke of a "crusade," only to later retract the term — and Osama Bin Laden, have described this confrontation in terms of a clash of civilizations and even as a religious war. "The world has been divided into two camps," Bin Laden asserted, "one under the banner of the cross, as the chief of the infidels, Bush, has stated, and the other under the banner of Islam."[21] Attacked for the first time within its own borders,[22] in a particularly brutal act aimed at the heart of its greatest metropolis, the United States decided to respond by breaking with international agreements and going it alone. Fearing a rash and impulsive reaction, the world held its breath. The emergence of the secretary of state, Colin Powell, as the most lucid personality in the U.S. Administration,[23] allowed the United States to maintain its sangfroid. It made the most of the emotion and international solidarity expressed by almost every foreign ministry (with Iraq as a notable exception) in order to reinforce its planetary hegemony.

With the disappearance of the Soviet Union in December 1991, it was clear that the United States had become the one and only hyperpower, even if some dissenters — *inter alia* Russia, China and in its own way, France — resisted admitting it. The events of September 11 broke down all such resistance; Moscow, Beijing, Paris and many other capitals around the world explicitly recognized the supremacy of the United States. A great number of leaders — first among them, the French President Jacques Chirac — hastened to Washington to offer their official condolences. In reality, they went to submit their unconditional vassalage. Everyone understood that the time of denial was over. President Bush had warned that anyone who was not with the United States was with the terrorists, adding that anyone who remained passive at that particular moment would be remembered.

Once universal compliance had been established — and this included the United Nations, NATO and the European Union — Washington behaved in an arrogant fashion, riding roughshod over the recommendations or wishes of its supporter countries. The coalition took shape, obeying a variable structure in which Washington elected its partner at any given moment, unilaterally setting the mission that was to be accomplished with no room for comment. As one U.S. analyst noted, European participation in the war would be on the basis of a unilateral arrangement that demanded the clear acceptance of only one authority: the U.S. high command.[24]

This was not only applicable in the military terrain. In terms of information — the "invisible war" — more than 50 countries placed their intelligence and counterespionage services under the orders of the CIA and the FBI. Thanks to this, within a matter of weeks, more than 360 people had been detained around the world under suspicion of having links with Bin Laden's al-Qaida network.[25]

The supremacy of the United States was already immense. Now it has become overwhelming. The U.S. political analyst, William Pfaff, noted that, at the start of 2002, the world was in a situation without precedent in the history of humanity. A single nation, the

United States, had unrivaled military and economic power and could impose its will wherever it wished. Even without resorting to nuclear weapons, the United States could destroy the military forces of any other nation on Earth. If it so desired, it could force total social and economic bankruptcy on any country. Pfaff concludes that no nation has ever wielded so much power nor been so invulnerable.[26] In comparison with the United States, the other western or westernized powers (France, Germany, Japan, Italy, Canada and the United Kingdom) are lilliputian figures. The most resounding proof of the U.S. power of intimidation was displayed no later than the day after September 11.

BIN LADEN'S STRATEGY

In organizing the September 9, 2001, assassination of Commander Massud, the military chief of the Northern Alliance, Osama Bin Laden believed that he had eliminated one of the most decisive weapons Washington could have used after the attacks. The United States, he thought, could not go on using the Northern Alliance for support. If it persisted in the aim of overthrowing the Taliban regime as protectors of al-Qaida, it would end up in confrontation with Pakistan. Let us recall that Pakistan is a redoubtable military power, in possession of nuclear weapons and with a population of 150 million people. Bin Laden believed that Islamabad would never agree to the dismantling of the Taliban regime, as it had allowed Pakistan to make an ancestral dream come true: at last it controlled Afghanistan, which had effectively been reduced to the status of a protectorate.

Further to the north, Russia was still in a standoff with Washington because of their serious disagreement over President Bush's cherished antimissile shield project. Therefore, it would not collaborate with the United States, nor would it offer any intermediation with its close allies in Central Asia, Uzbekistan and Tajikistan.

According to this commonsense reasoning, the United States would have to resign itself to bombing Afghanistan from afar after September 11. Bill Clinton had had to do just that in 1998 after the attacks against the U.S. embassies in Nairobi and Dar es Salaam. While his response was certainly spectacular, there were no real results.

As the course of events has shown, Osama Bin Laden was wrong. The Pakistani high command and the president-general, Pervez Musharraf, was faced with the inescapable dilemma of siding with the United States or taking considerable risks in such high-priority strategic concerns as Kashmir, rivalry with India and possession of nuclear weapons. In less than 24 hours, they opted, as is well known, to sacrifice Afghanistan.

Russia did not vacillate either. On September 11, Vladimir Putin was the first to contact Bush to express his solidarity. As far away as he was in Central Asia, the top brass of the U.S. Army could only be moved by the gesture. Moscow's reward for this has been two-fold: the silence of the United States about the atrocities committed by the Russian Army in its "fight against terrorism" in Chechnya, and the agreement to Russia becoming a de facto member of NATO.[27]

Moscow's change of attitude clearly means that there is no longer the possibility of constituting a military coalition that could act as a counterbalance to the United States. Today, its military preeminence is absolute. The "punishment" visited upon Afghanistan after October 7, with bombing raids day and night for several months, is therefore a terrifying warning for the rest of the world. Anyone who dares oppose the United States will do so alone, without a single ally, clearly running the risk of being bombed back into the stone age. The list of the next potential "targets" has been publicly announced in U.S. newspapers: Somalia, Yemen, Sudan, Iraq, Iran, Syria, North Korea and Cuba. In his State of the Union address on January 29, 2002, President Bush, brandishing the "Axis of Evil," explicitly named three targets: North Korea, Iran and, in particular, Iraq.

Another lesson in the wake of September 11 is that globalization is gathering strength as the main characteristic of the contemporary world. Yet the present crisis has also revealed its vulnerability. The United States consequently maintains that the setting up of some sort of globalized security apparatus is an urgent priority.

The pretext of the worldwide struggle to combat terrorism has enabled freedoms to be curtailed and the perimeters of democracy to be reduced the world over.[28] With this, combined with Russia's participation and China's entry into the WTO, it would seem that everything is in place for such global security measures to be carried out.[29] Whether this occurs under the auspices of the new NATO or, more probably, under the direct control of the U.S. Armed Forces, remains to be seen. The fact is that these measures, under the pretext of "combating terrorism," are already being directly implemented, on such far-flung fronts as the Philippines, Afghanistan, Pakistan, Georgia, Yemen, Somalia and Colombia. This has given rise to the idea that we have entered a new period of contemporary history where, once again, political problems can be fixed with military solutions.

There are also voices saying that neoliberal globalization is partly responsible for the events of September 11, a consequence of the way it has exacerbated injustices, inequalities and poverty on a planetary scale.[30] The result is the growing desperation and rancor of millions who are prepared to rebel, such as those in the Arab Islamic world who will determinedly give their support to the most radical Islamic groups, including al-Qaida, that appeal to the most extreme forms of violence. Undermining states, devaluing politics and dismantling the main sets of rules, globalization has favored the formation of organizations that are flexible in structure, nonhierarchical, non-vertical and reticular. Both global enterprises and NGOs have taken advantage of the new status quo and have multiplied.

These same conditions, however, have also given rise to parasite organizations, surging chaotically into spaces degraded by globalization: mafia groups, criminal organizations and crime rings of all kinds, sects and terrorist groups.[31] Understood from this perspective, the network-sect of al-Qaida is an organization that is perfectly adapted to the era of globalization. It has multinational branches, finance networks, media and communications connections, economic resources, sources of supply, teaching and training centers, humanitarian organizations, organs of propaganda, subsidiaries and sub-subsidiaries.

Throughout history, the world has known city-states (Athens, Sparta, Venice, Hong Kong, Singapore etc.); region-states (in the feudal period, but also in contemporary times, with decentralization, autonomous regions and neofederalism); party-states (Mussolini's fascist party in Italy, Hitler's national-socialism in Germany, the communist party in Stalin's Soviet Union); and nation-states (in the 19th and 20th centuries).

With globalization, however, we are witnessing the emergence of the network-state, and even the individual-state, of which Osama Bin Laden is the first clear example. Nonetheless, for the moment, the latter continues to need — just as the hermit crab needs an empty shell — an "empty state" to appropriate (Somalia, Afghanistan) before putting it to the fullest use in the service of his ambitions.

Globalization already favors this phenomenon, just as it will come to favor the appearance of the enterprise-state in the very near future. Just as Bin Laden and al-Qaida have done, some global enterprise will take over a hollow, empty, destructured state, prisoner of endemic disorder and chaos, to use it at its whim. In this case also, Osama Bin Laden will somehow have been a horrific forerunner.

THE MIDDLE EAST
THE NEW HUNDRED YEARS WAR

In September 2003, two years after the tragic attacks of September 11, 2001, with the U.S. offensive against the Taliban regime and Osama Bin Laden's al-Qaida network complete, and with military victory in Iraq, the "hundred years war" between the Israelis and Palestinians continues to ravage the Middle East. There seems to be no solution to the war between Israel and Palestine, the "black hole" of international politics.

By February 2002, the "second Intifada" and the subsequent Israeli repression had already caused more than 1,000 deaths (over 260 Israelis and about 915 Palestinians). This figure does not include the thousands of wounded on both sides, many of whom have been disabled for the rest of their lives.

In these dramatic circumstances, let us not forget the words pronounced by Itzhak Rabin before he too was felled by the bullets of a fanatical Jewish killer, "We, the soldiers who have come back from combat covered in blood, we, who have struggled against you, the Palestinians, we say to you today, loud and clear, 'Enough tears have been shed and enough blood spilled. Enough!'"

Nonetheless, in the seven years since his death, blood and tears continue to rain on the martyred lands of Israel and Palestine! On September 28, 2000, General Ariel Sharon's appearance on the Esplanade of the Mosques (Temple Mount to the Jews) provoked another tragic sequence of events: protests by Palestinian civilians lead to disproportionate Israeli brutality,[1] in which Palestinian adolescents and children were mowed down by Israeli bullets. What followed: two Israeli soldiers were horrendously lynched, mutilated and burned; there were reprisals against Arab Israelis, there were suicide attacks in the streets of Israeli cities, the military reoccupied the autonomous Palestinian cities, there were provocations by extremist settlers and new and detestable attacks against Israeli civilians, etc. The spiral of violence seems endless.

The worldwide shock of September 11, 2001, did not stop this cycle of revenge. Rather, it seems to have increased the intensity, especially after Operation Protective Shield, comprising the Separation Wall, was launched in March and April 2002. In response to a number of particularly cruel Palestinian attacks, the Israeli Army destroyed part of the West Bank city of Jenin.[2]

Routine barbarism. This is a political regression to the ethnic-religious conflicts of Bosnia, Kosovo and Chechnya, where fanatics on both sides call for "ethnic cleansing" or "segregation of populations."[3] It is a return to despair for Palestinian civilians, whose living conditions have become infernal thanks to the successive blockades of their cities.[4] It is also a return to unease and fear for a traumatized and tormented Israeli society, where, nonetheless, the majority continues to favor a peace agreement.[5] What a tragic disappointment for those who thought they had seen the end to a century of conflict with the 1993 Oslo Peace Accords!

SETBACKS

Itzhak Rabin's murder was the first major setback to the peace process. Later, in 1996, Binyamin Netanyahu was elected by a population still in a state of shock after a series of attacks by Islamic fundamentalists. As prime minister, Netanyahu brought about the definitive demise of the peace process, blocking negotiations, sabotaging the Oslo Peace Accords and violating UN resolutions. By implementing blockades and encouraging colonization by Jewish settlers, he exacerbated the harsh material conditions of the Palestinians. Such intolerable living conditions frequently pushed Palestinians to join armed organizations that were also hostile to the Oslo Peace Accords and in favor of terrorism.

In Gaza, for example, a million Palestinians are crowded together in conditions of indescribable squalor, while 6,000 extremist Jewish settlers, protected by soldiers who are armed to the teeth, occupy a third of the territory, which includes the best-irrigated land. In contempt of international law, Netanyahu encouraged the introduction of Jewish populations in the Arab quarter of Jerusalem, often consisting of people who had arrived from other countries. His policy toward the Palestinians was humiliation and repression. Netanyahu has been condemned by the United Nations and denounced by the Jewish human rights organization Betselem for using torture as a political weapon. The newspaper *Haaretz* described Israel as "the only state in the world that has legally enshrined torture, completely officially."[6]

ISRAEL, A MORAL PROJECT

The colonial and repressive stance of the Israeli authorities is abhorrent to many Israeli citizens. This state is unlike any other in the world, being the fruit of the Zionist theses formulated in 1896 by Theodor Herlz. According to the Israeli historian, Zeev Sternhell, Zionism is essentially none other than "a classical variant of the closed nationalism that appeared in Europe at the close of the 19th century... It has no objection to denying the very same basic rights that it demands for itself with total aplomb."

It is also undeniable that the state of Israel emerged from European anti-Semitism, the Russian pogroms and Nazi genocide. It constitutes both a gateway and a haven for millions of persecuted and discriminated who seek a space that offers them peace and freedom.[7] For these people, and the death camp survivors in particular, Israel is not merely a national project but a moral project as well.

It is, however, a moral project that has been betrayed, as should be evident even to those who persist in ignoring the terrible abuses committed by the Israelis. A group of scholars known as the "New Historians" of Israel, with irrefutable proof in their hands, have cast doubt on the blamelessness of their state.[8] Even official Israeli television finally admitted the historical truth in 1998 when a documentary series called "Tekouma" (Rebirth) revealed to the public the essential falsity of the colonial slogan "a land without people for a people without land."

DISCRIMINATION AND REPRISALS

In 1948, Israeli soldiers conducted widespread massacres in order to terrorize the Palestinians and encourage them to flee, as has been recorded in a number of hair-raising documentaries. Those Palestinians who remained in Israel today number more than a million (15 percent of them Christians), constituting a sixth of the country's population. While they are submitted to less discrimination today than previously (they were subject to military authority until 1966), they continue to be second-class citizens. This, despite the promises made in the Declaration of Independence (read by David Ben Gurion on May 14, 1948) to the effect that the state of Israel would "uphold the full social and political equality of all its citizens, without distinction of race, creed or sex."

This commitment has never been put into practise and the rights of the Arab Israeli citizens have never been respected, as was tragically demonstrated by the racist reprisals in Galilee at the beginning of October 2000. When Arab Israelis protested against repression in the West Bank and Gaza, 13 victims were killed, in Nazareth and other places, when the military fired on protesters using live ammunition. Actual pogroms were organized by thugs from Likud and other ultraright political parties.

Yet on the night of his electoral triumph in May 1999, the Labor prime minister, Ehud Barak, promised to set out again on the road to peace. Was he not the man who dared to say, in April 1998, thoroughly scandalizing the right, "If I were a young Palestinian, I too would opt for violence"? Indeed, Barak decided to end the military occupation of Southern Lebanon. In this strip of territory, the hasty withdrawal of the Israeli Army and the rather inglorious departure of the South Lebanon Army (SLA) were interpreted by Hizbullah (the Shi'ite fundamentalist militia supported by Iran) and part of Arab public opinion as a great military victory over Israel, the first in half a century of Israeli-Arab confrontations.

For a moment it appeared that hopes of seeing a successful conclusion to the peace negotiations had faded and that the region would enter yet another cycle of instability and tension. Things, as always in the Middle East, could still get worse. Appearances, however, were deceptive. The Middle East was longing for peace. Israeli public opinion called for it loud and clear, and a certain realism prevailed in most Arab countries. In addition, the time had come for many Arab countries to change their leaders. A new generation had taken over the leadership in Jordan and Syria, while the question of succession continues to be crucial in Saudi Arabia, Egypt and within the Palestinian Authority. None of the old leaders wish to leave war as their legacy.

REFORM IN IRAN

In Iran, the country that provides shelter for the Lebanese Hizbullah militia, those who favor reform within their country continue to gain ground. If solidarity toward the Palestinians continues to be a "national cause," this solidarity does not necessarily involve exclusive support for armed struggle and terrorist attacks against Israel, according to the reformers.

Indeed, the winds of freedom have been blowing in Iran since the overwhelming victory of the Iran Participation Front in the parliamentary election of February 8, 2000. The majority of the seats in parliament went to the reformer friends of President Mohammed Jatami. Following the triumphs of the presidential (May 1997) and municipal (March 1999) elections, this upheaval at the urns confirmed the intensity of the Iranian society's demand for change 24 years after the Islamic revolution.

Events in this country, three times bigger than Spain and populated by 66 million people, have a worldwide significance. Iran's future directly concerns the entire Muslim world, which encompasses over a billion human beings and covers land from Morocco to Indonesia and from Kosovo to Nigeria.

Fueled by egalitarianism, Third World solidarity, anti-Zionism and anti-Americanism, Iranian Islamic ideas have spread throughout the Muslim world since 1979. In every country and, in particular, among the most disadvantaged sectors, Iran aimed to establish networks that would favor the coming to power of hard-line Muslims. By doing so, Iran aspired to become the overall leader of a combative political Islam that would oppose Saudi Arabian traditionalism.

The project failed. Today, the revolutionary regime is in total disarray. It is despised for its widespread corruption, fractured by serious internal discord, discredited by its repressive excesses and criticized for its reactionary conformism with regard to traditions. Its three big successes are in the social, educational and democratic spheres: the revolution benefited the dispossessed; it has provided literacy campaigns and free education for all, while more than two million students — mainly women — have been offered places in higher education; and the elections of May 1997, March 1999 and February 2000 were carried out with total transparency.

Paradoxically, these three achievements have aggravated the regime's disrepute. Now profoundly transformed, educated and politicized, members of the younger generation are expressing their frustration. Once again the celebrated axiom of Tocqueville is relevant: "when great revolutions are successful their causes cease to exist, and the fact of their success has made them incomprehensible for new generations."[9]

Women, young people, intellectuals and the reform camp are calling for a revolution within the revolution. In his own way, President Mohammed Jatami is reminiscent of Mikhail Gorbachev who, as head of the Soviet Union, called for transparency (*glasnost*) and reorganization (*perestroika*) in the regime that emerged from the 1917 revolution.

Nonetheless, Jatami's followers do not turn their backs on the 1979 events and still less do they dream of restoration. If they say "no" to the mullahs' regime, it is because they oppose the hijacking of the revolution by a Shi'ite clergy that is incapable of giving new drive to the country.

THE END OF A THEOCRACY

Rethinking the theocratic character of the Islamic republic is the crux of the debate between conservatives and reformers.[10] The entire Muslim world is following this debate expectantly. The reformers sustain that the institution of *velayat faguih* (literally, "the teaching of the religious guide") which establishes the authority of a nonelected "supreme guide" (at the time of writing, Ayatollah Ali Khamenei) over that of the democratically elected president of the republic, does not have divine legitimacy. This is not only the stance of lay people but also of many high-ranking religious personalities. Already aware of the discredited status of the clergy, and aware that mosque attendance is suffering, they fear that Islam itself will suffer because of the unpopularity of the regime.

Reformers are therefore campaigning to end the all-embracing power of religious dogma, in exchange for the establishment of democracy, a multiparty system, freedom of opinion, the right of intellectuals and artists to criticize and better access for women to senior positions. They express their concerns, not without risk, in hundreds of new newspapers and reviews that testify to the intellectual effervescence and formidable creativity in the country. In the economic domain, however, projects are more vague. The situation is alarming, with 20 percent unemployment, more than 50 percent of the population below the poverty line and a foreign debt of more than $22 billion. While some are in favor of conserving a strong public sector, especially with regard to fossil fuels, others call for privatization of all nationalized companies and even for the liquidation of state monopolies in the transport, telecommunications and energy spheres. The reform camp, while it may be united against the conservatives, is divided over basic issues.

So the swords are still flashing. The conservatives, led by their "supreme guide" Ali Khamenei, continue to control the judiciary, the mass media, the economy, the police, the armed forces and the paramilitary militia. The possibility of confrontation between the two sides cannot be discounted. Jatami and his modernizing friends should note: history teaches that the most dangerous moment to embark upon reform is precisely when a nation is emerging from a long period of conservatism.

Ironically, the attacks of September 11, 2001, and the war on Afghanistan, paved the way for Teheran's reinsertion into the diplomatic sphere of the international order. As an enemy of the Taliban regime and a protector of the Hazara (Shi'ite) minority in Afghanistan, Iran is, in fact, one of the beneficiaries of the new situation created by the fall of the Taliban. Evidently, this new situation favored a rapprochement between Teheran and Washington. The thawing in relations, however, was unceremoniously interrupted in January 2002 when, in his State of the Union address, President Bush unexpectedly included Iran, along with Iraq and North Korea, as one of the countries constituting the "Axis of Evil."

This transformed context, while not implying less commitment by Iran toward the creation of a Palestinian state, should lead Teheran to prioritize diplomatic action rather than exclusive support to Hizbullah and other organizations that support violence and terrorism against Israel in their efforts to achieve a liberated Palestine.

NEGOTIATING WITH SYRIA

Why, after taking 22 years to think about it, did the government of Israel suddenly decide to apply UN Security Council Resolution 425, which urged it to withdraw its troops from Southern Lebanon? First, after his triumph in the May 1999 election, Ehud Barak promised to end an occupation that was very unpopular in Israel. Again, from a strictly military point of view, the occupation did not in the least guarantee the security of Israel and its population. More importantly, however, the withdrawal of the troops would enable negotiations with Syria to be renewed.

After his election, these negotiations were Ehud Barak's priority. He was prepared to return the essential part of Golan Heights to Damascus, an offer already formulated by his predecessors, confirming his wish to make progress in reaching an agreement with Damascus. As is well known, however, this commitment fell apart because of the insistence of the former Syrian president, Hafez al-Assad, on obtaining — in addition to what had been agreed in the UN Security Council Resolution 242 — a return to the ceasefire lines established on June 4, 1967, thereby giving Syria access to the eastern shore of the Sea of Galilee.

In withdrawing from Southern Lebanon without having managed to reach agreement with Damascus, Barak had three objectives: he was giving further proof to the international community of his desire for peace; he was depriving Damascus of its prestigious role as Hizbullah's protector, whose blows to the Israeli troops were celebrated throughout the Muslim Arab world; and finally, he was pointing the finger at "the other occupation" of the Land of the Cedars — because Syria has 35,000 troops deployed on Lebanese soil. In one move, he obliged the Syrians to reflect: if they permitted Hizbullah to act inside Israel, they would be liable to suffer the consequences.

Damascus could hardly have afforded this. The country was sinking quickly. Any major crisis would have seriously jeopardized President Assad's main concern: ensuring that his son would succeed him. On the other hand, an agreement with Israel would have numerous advantages for Syria. It would recover the Golan Heights, conserve its strategic interests in Lebanon and gain access to loans from the West. For both sides, the die was cast for agreement.

LOST OPPORTUNITY

In spite of the bloody clashes of May 2000, there were several signs indicating that, seven years after the Oslo Accords, a historic agreement would soon be reached between Israel and Palestine, concerning the three main bones of contention: the territories, Jerusalem and refugees. Secret negotiations held in Stockholm from the beginning of May, between Shlomo Ben Ami, then the Israeli minister of public security, and Ahmed Qorei (Abu Allah), speaker of the Palestinian Legislative Council, had considerable surprises in store, from both parties. Israel would have ceded between 90 percent and 92 percent of the West Bank (and not between 60 percent and 75 percent as was expected), excluding the region of Jerusalem. The Palestinians would have to leave the territories where about 80 percent of the Jewish settlers resided.

In the case of Jerusalem, the Palestinians would have been able to move their capital to Abu Dis, a neighborhood of the holy city recently returned by Israel that would thereafter have been called al-Quds, the Arab name of the city. Al-Quds would also be connected with the holy Muslim sites by means of a passageway under Palestinian control. East Jerusalem, with its population of 200,000 Palestinians, would have remained under Israeli sovereignty, but the municipal administration would have been Palestinian.

Finally, with regard to the delicate issue of the refugees (almost four million Palestinians), Israel would have permitted the symbolic return of a few dozen people while offering reparations to the rest. It was this point, and particularly the Palestinians' appeal to the "right of return" as enshrined in the UN General Assembly Resolution 194 of December 11, 1948, that constituted the main stumbling block. The possibility of "postponing" the matter for future negotiations between the state of Palestine and the state of Israel was then raised.

PEACE WITHIN ARM'S REACH

After his valiant decision to end the occupation of Southern Lebanon and his equally bold intention to return Golan to Syria, Ehud Barak seemed determined to end the injustices that were being perpetrated against the Palestinians. These developments made peace appear to be within arm's reach. It seemed that agreement on the main problem areas — restitution of territories, East Jerusalem and the refugees — would soon be reached.[11]

This therefore implied — for both parties, but especially the Palestinians — a series of concessions that extremists on both sides described as "unacceptable," if not "sacrilegious." In short, seven years after the Oslo agreement, for all its imperfections, at last seemed solid enough to relaunch true progress toward peace. Eradicating violence in the region, this process would guarantee the legitimate Israeli aspiration for security, while recognizing the equally legitimate Palestinian right to live in a sovereign state. It would thus permit the Middle East to get on with the fundamental work of democratic, economic and social development.

When peace had been so close, how is it possible that now, at the threshold of the 21st century, Israelis and Palestinians are still immersed in this infernal war? New revelations about the secret negotiations at Camp David (United States) in June 2000, have shown that the Palestinians, indignant about the constant violations of the Israeli authorities, were not willing to make any further substantial concessions. It is true that, in recognizing Israel on November 15, 1988, their National Council had accepted that the Jewish state would occupy 78 percent of Mandated Palestine, accepting that the remaining 22 percent would form the state of Palestine. In these circumstances, how could they also be expected to concede 10 percent of the West Bank? This land to be returned to Palestine did not include the Jerusalem region or the Jordan Valley, which Barak wished to keep under Israeli sovereignty. A further hindrance to negotiations was that the map drafted by the Israeli delegation had cut the West Bank of the River Jordan into three discontinuous zones. Is it not a fact that the UN Security Council Resolution 242, adopted in 1967, demanded Israeli withdrawal from the occupied territories? Weren't the Oslo Accords based on the surrender of land in exchange for peace?

In addition, the Palestinians were not prepared to give way on the issue of East Jerusalem, the city they intended to make their capital. They considered that international law was on their side, since Resolution 242 required Israel to withdraw from the pre-1967 war borders. Nonetheless, as a demonstration of goodwill, they agreed to give Israel total authority over the Wailing Wall, and also — a basic concession — authority over the Jewish neighborhoods in the old city.

Ehud Barak, feeling that he was the representative of the will of his people for whom a reunified Jerusalem should continue to be the "eternal capital" of Israel, could not make the concession of recognizing Palestinian sovereignty over the eastern part of the city. In turn, Yasser Arafat, considering himself to be the person in whom all the faithful and Muslim states had vested the duty of safeguarding Islam's holy places, could hardly let his arm be twisted either.

This double impasse over a political issue weighed down by a heavy religious component, was destined to frustrate negotiations. In September 2000, Barak offered to agree to the Palestinian capital being established less than two kilometers from the Esplanade of the Mosques, and for it to remain under Palestinian guardianship (but not sovereignty). However, his final proposals were not sufficient to detain the machinery of violence, which simply went into high gear when General Ariel Sharon came to power.

RIGHT OF RETURN?

Another burning issue: the fate of the refugees of 1948 — whose forced exodus has been reconstructed by the "New Historians" of Israel — and those of 1967. In this regard also, international law was on the side of the Palestinians. On December 11, 1948, the United Nations established their right of return and the state of Israel formally recognized it. In fact, at the Lausanne Conference, on May 12,

1949, Israel and its Arab neighbors signed a protocol accepting both the 1947 partition plan and Resolution 194. The entry of Israel into the United Nations on this same day, May 12, 1949, meant that the agreement made in Lausanne was not worth the paper it was written on. Walter Eytan, joint head of the Israeli Ministry of Foreign Affairs, subsequently recognized that his main objective was actually to undermine the protocol of May 12, which Israel had been obliged to sign in its struggle to become a member of the United Nations.[12]

Fifty years later, Israel has "forgotten" about this episode. It believes that the return of the refugees constitutes a threat to its Jewish character and its very existence. Accordingly, the least Ehud Barak could do at Camp David was to make some move in the direction of Yasser Arafat. Nonetheless, intellectual honesty requires one to recognize that, in this dispute as in the rest, the Palestine Authority is partly responsible. It failed to present its own proposals, or its objections to the Israeli proposals, in clear enough terms before, during and after the Camp David summit. It is also true that the Israeli leaders and mass media manipulated the issue of the right of return for their own purposes.

Even the great Israeli writer and veteran of the peace movement, Amos Oz, has gone so far as to write:

> [Recognition of this right] is the same as abolishing the right to self-determination of the Jewish people. It will turn the Jewish people into an ethnic minority at the mercy of the Arabs, into a "protected minority," just as the Muslim fundamentalists wanted. Recognizing the "right of return" goes hand in hand with the destruction of Israel. Instead of "two states for two nations," what will appear in this land in the end will be two Arab states.[13]

Would this scaremongering have been as effective if, following the example of Leila Shahid, the Palestinian Liberation Organization (PLO) representative in France, the Palestinian leader had refrained from publicly stating (while his negotiators were doing so behind closed doors) that, "It is evident that nobody wants to modify the

Jewish nature of the state of Israel... It is evident that the right of return cannot be applied to all the refugees. Accordingly, its application will have to be negotiated, but it is no less evident that the right must be recognized"?[14]

THE TABA AGREEMENT

Whatever the case, these irreconcilable differences should not have served to justify the opinion of some observers that at Camp David, Ehud Barak had made a "generous offer," which Yasser Arafat had obstinately rejected. There can be no doubt that the Israeli prime minister went further than any of his predecessors, yet it was not far enough to satisfy the stipulations of international law and to create the *sine qua non* conditions for establishing a viable and independent state of Palestine. "It was not possible," say these same observers; history will be the judge. The Israeli Government and the Palestine Authority eventually agreed to resume the negotiations they had begun in the United States on the basis of new guidelines: suggestions made by President Clinton, published in December 2000. These negotiations took place in the Egyptian city of Taba. We now know that these negotiations allowed the drawing up of the general outlines of a possible agreement on all the disputed points, including the right of return, in exchange for "flexible application."[15]

Meanwhile, Israeli Prime Minister Ehud Barak had stepped down, which occasioned the early elections held on February 6, 2001. Given that Ariel Sharon's victory was on the cards, Barak considered that the Israeli-Palestinian entente no longer worked in favor of his possible reelection, but had instead become a millstone around his neck. He therefore withdrew his negotiators. What if, instead of throwing in the towel, Barak had given himself a few months to produce a polished agreement and then defended it before Israeli public opinion? Available data leads one to think that a clear majority of Israelis would have approved, as long as peace could exist in conditions of security and respect, with both countries free to decide their own destinies. Unfortunately, this is now mere conjecture. The election of the Likud president, Ariel Sharon, led to bloodstained confrontations and the dramatic impasse facing the region since the end of 2001.

THE RESPONSIBILITY OF THE UNITED STATES

The United States has a great deal of responsibility in the evolution of this process: instead of acting as a mediator, it has constantly displayed its bias toward Israel. Meanwhile, it has persistently threatened military action against a number of Arab countries (Yemen, Sudan and of course Iraq) accused by Washington of harboring, protecting and helping Islamic terrorist organizations after the attacks of September 11, 2001.

For a period of several weeks at the end of 2001, at the height of the military offensive against Afghanistan, the U.S. mass media circulated the rumor that the Pentagon was about to launch an attack on Iraq. This nation had been (unjustly) accused of causing the anthrax panic that spread like wildfire across the country in the days that followed September 11. The impression that the United States was attempting to take advantage of the international crisis in order to settle a problem still unsolved since the Gulf War was strong.

Many of Israel's diehard friends called upon the United States to take this path. They were well aware, in this unipolar world, that the United States is the most powerful voice in the international order and is capable of wielding its hegemony in an authoritarian fashion.

The fact is that the United States is subjugating the world as no other empire in the entire history of humanity has ever done. Is it not the case that after its victory in the 1991 Gulf War, Washington proposed a New World Order fashioned in its own image? In prophetic tones, President George Bush Snr. declared that the United States had been called upon to bring the world out of the darkness and chaos of dictatorships and to lead it toward the promise of better times. This desire to play the part of world leader, intervening in crises to tip the balance toward the side more favorable to U.S. interests, was only confirmed during Bill Clinton's presidential mandate. "The United States considers that it has been charged with a mission, one it has assigned to itself thanks to its presence on the world stage," noted Hubert Védrine, the French minister for foreign affairs. "What we are faced with is the phenomenon of a hyper-power."[16]

Former Secretary of State Madeleine Albright had already reminded the world, in the context of the February 1998 confrontation with Iraq, that she represented "an America that is totally convinced of having global responsibilities. This means that when we can change things, we must do so."[17] This meant bypassing the United Nations where Washington, in rejecting Butros Butros Ghali's election in 1996, had imposed the condition that the new secretary general should not be a politician. "The UN secretary general," decreed Ms. Albright, "must be just an administrator. It is possible that [he or she] might play a more political role in some future historical period, but not in the next five years."[18] The irony of history has determined that this "administrator" should be Kofi Annan, who with his performance in different crises, has shown the need for politics — and for the United Nations.

NO STRATEGY FOR THE MIDDLE EAST

Apart from its unwavering support for Israel, the United States does not have any clear overall strategy for the Middle East. Washington has taken no decisive step to revive the peace negotiations between the Israelis and Palestinians, not even after the attacks of September 11. Sending General Anthony Zinn as mediator was a minor diplomatic measure. The present situation in the Arab world, however, differs from that which existed in 1991 at the time of the first Gulf War. The brutality of the embargo imposed on Baghdad (for the last 11 years, Iraqi children have been dying at a rate of one every six minutes) and the U.S. bombing attacks of 1992, 1993, 1996 and 1998 give the impression of an anti-Iraq fury with civilians as its main victims.

In contrast, the attitude of the United States is exceptionally indulgent with regard to the Israeli authorities, a country that continues to occupy part of Syria (Golan), the territories of Gaza and the West Bank, and East Jerusalem, in flagrant contempt of international law. It is a country where Ariel Sharon, turning a deaf ear to protests, decided to put an end to the peace negotiations with the Palestinians and to step up colonization and repression. In short, it is a country which possesses the whole battery of weapons of mass destruction (WMD) — chemical, biological and atomic — and which for the last 30 years has been violating all UN resolutions that refer to it. It has never once been sanctioned. On the contrary, Washington continues to grant giant aid packages, year after year, to the tune of $3 billion.

This situation was perceived as a tremendous injustice in Arab public opinion, which responded with increasingly forceful expressions of sympathy for the people of Iraq. Without overlooking the fact that the Baghdad regime was a dictatorship based on terror and repression, the leading intellectuals of the Arab world took the lead in a crusade of solidarity with Iraqi society. Fearing the power of this movement (and in protest against the intransigence of the government of Israel), most of the region's leaders refused to support U.S. plans to bomb Iraq after its Afghanistan victory in January 2002.

JUSTICE DENIED

The United States has never been able to respond firmly to the intransigence of the Israeli authorities. They could not even do so in March 2002, when the Arab Summit in Beirut unanimously proposed the adoption of the peace initiative proposed by the Saudi Arabian crown prince, based on the idea of land-for-peace: total peace in exchange for all the territories occupied by Israel since June 1967. Although Washington officially supported this plan and President Bush spoke of the need for a "Palestinian state," he did not protest when Prime Minister Sharon embarked on his Separation Wall offensive in response to this proposal. Sharon sent 75,000 soldiers to reoccupy the West Bank, with a toll of dozens of deaths and inestimable destruction. The stakes are not equal. All those who frenetically call for "balance" in the media treatment of this confrontation are only trying to mask the pure truth.[19]

It could not be clearer: in the West Bank and Gaza we have a blatant miscarriage of justice in terms of the basic rights of the Palestinians. In my view, this denial of justice in no way justifies resorting to blind terrorism and indiscriminate attacks against innocent Israeli civilians. Palestinian leaders who opt for terrorism continue to ignore the democratic character of an Israeli society that freely elects its leaders. The more terrified they are, the more Israelis tend to vote in favor of their hard-line and intransigent leaders. It is time that a nonviolent and powerful movement appeared in Palestinian society, with the objective of working hand in hand with the Israeli pacifist movement. All the opinion polls show that there is a majority of citizens on both sides who, in spite of everything that has happened, want to progress toward peace and reconciliation.

In any other part of the world, a situation of repression approximating this one would have provoked the righteous indignation of intellectuals who, in other such cases, raise their voices against human rights violations. We have witnessed them calling for the creation of international courts, alerting public opinion (as in the cases of Kosovo, Chechnya and East Timor), even demanding military intervention. "Many intellectuals — for example, Daniel Bensaid, Rony Brauman and Marcel-Francis Kahn, who are committed to the defense of the national rights of Bosnians, Chechnyans and Kosovars — are at best strangely silent when it comes to Palestinian refugees and camps."[20]

Israel, the military superpower riding on the coat-tails of the U.S. hyperpower, must show that it can be just. Its political leadership, bereft of imagination, daring and spirit for some time now, seems incapable of confronting the challenges posed by post-Zionism. Will they have the nerve to make the indispensable concessions? To dismantle the colonies embedded in places like Gaza and Hebron and illegally created by ultraright racist fanatics who are armed to the teeth? To abandon their delusion that the Palestinians will always accept whatever goes, because the balance of power is so blatantly against them? To admit that the Palestinians are struggling for their freedom and independence and that the occupation, while unjust to the Palestinians, is suicide for the state of Israel?[21]

TRUTH AND RECONCILIATION

For many reasons, the Middle East cannot afford to continually postpone the resolution of this conflict. In Israel, as in Palestine, public opinion is calling for it. The solution, which must be political, must entail the peaceful and even constructive coexistence of the Jewish and Arab states. Equally, it requires reconciliation between the two peoples, each of whom must come to terms with their own history.

The importance of the call made five years ago by Edward Said resides in this point. This U.S. intellectual of Palestinian origin replied as follows to the Arab friends of Roger Garaudy:

> The thesis that the Holocaust is no more than a Zionist fraud is beginning to circulate in different circles in a deplorable fashion. How can we expect the world to become aware of our sufferings as Arabs if we show that we are incapable of recognizing the suffering of others, even if it is that of our oppressors, and if we show that we are incapable of accepting the facts when they contradict the simplistic ideas of holier-than-thou intellectuals who refuse to see the relation that exists between the Holocaust and Israel? Saying that we must be conscious of the reality of the Holocaust does not in any way mean accepting that the Holocaust excuses Zionism of the harm it has done to Palestinians. On the contrary, recognizing the history of the Holocaust and the insanity of the genocide of the Jewish people makes us credible with regard to our own history; it permits us to ask the Israelis and the Jews to establish the connection between the Holocaust and the injustices that Zionism has perpetrated against the Palestinians, to make this connection and at the same time question it, for what it conceals in hypocrisy and moral debasement.

To give credence to the thesis of Roger Garaudy and his negationist friends in the name of "freedom of expression" is a cretinous ruse that only serves to discredit us in the eyes of the world. It is proof of a basic ignorance of the history of the world in which we live, a sign of incompetence and an inability to fight fairly.[22]

Other intellectuals in the Arab world have responded to this call, confronting the new outbreak of anti-Semitism fuelled by the degeneration of the conflict and opposing those who deny the Nazi genocide of the European Jews.

Perhaps this call can be seen as a hand stretched out across the river of blood currently separating the two peoples, in the hope of ushering in the day when truth will finally dissipate hatred, peace will endure and both peoples will be saved from the destruction that is foreshadowed.

GLOBALIZATION/ANTIGLOBALIZATION
PLANETARY SOCIAL WAR

4

Karl Marx once famously declared, "Give me the windmill and I'll give you the Middle Ages." We might paraphrase him to add, "Give me the steam engine and I'll give you the age of industry." Or, applying it to our own times, "Give me a computer and I'll give you globalization."

While such determinism is doubtless going a little too far, the basic idea is sound enough: at any of history's turning points, some new and brilliant invention has upset the status quo and set society off in a new direction, initiating a unique and long-lasting process. A little over a decade ago, we moved imperceptibly into such a phase.

At the end of the 18th century, the steam engine changed the face of the world, bringing about the Industrial Revolution. It led to the growth of capitalism, and gave rise to the working class, socialism, the expansion of colonialism, etc. Yet, all this machine did was replace muscle power. With the mission of replacing brain power, the computer is well on the way to bringing into being even more radical and unprecedented changes, before our very eyes. Anyone can see that everything around us is changing: the geopolitical framework, the economic context, political coordinates, ecological parameters, social values, cultural criteria and people's attitudes.

Information and communications technologies have combined with the digital revolution to force us recklessly into a new era, whose basic characteristics are the instantaneous transfer of immaterial data and the proliferation of electronic links and networks. The internet is the heart of the great transformation that is now underway. Information highways are to our times what the railways were to the industrial era: powerful elements that drive and intensify trade and commerce.

NEW ECONOMY

With this as their paradigm, many new investors recall that "the economic advantages of a transport system increase in fits and starts, making big leaps when specific connections are made," and that, "in the 1840s, the building of the railways was the single most significant spur to industrial growth in Western Europe."[1] Since the mid-1990s, neocapitalists have been gambling on the probability that this phase of economic lift-off will bring exponential growth in all activities related to information highways, virtual network technologies and the internet. In 1999 and 2000, this speculative fever came to be known as the "new economy."

Many investors were convinced that, as we experience one of the most rapid changes the world has ever known, companies would have to adapt and invest heavily in information technologies, digital phones, satellite telecommunications, etc. The prospects for growth in these sectors seemed boundless. In France, for instance, the figure for the possession of computer equipment in homes and offices doubled between 1997 and 2000. More than 10 million people acquired mobile phones in these three years. By December 31, 2001, the figure for mobile phone owners had reached 61.6 percent, meaning 37 million French people had mobile phones. Moreover, it was calculated that the global number of internet users, estimated at 142 million in 1998, would exceed 500 million in 2003.

The great economic battles of the future will see U.S., European and Japanese companies fighting to control the networks and take over the market of images, data, leisure, sound and games consoles. To sum up, it will be a fight for content itself. They will also be fighting for the domination of the predicted exponential development in the field of electronic commerce. Their logic has forced the internet to become a huge shopping mall.[2] In 1998, electronic business was still embryonic, with a turnover of some €8 billion; by 2000, it had reached €40 billion and the figure could be more than €80 million by 2005.

Driven by their fever for opulence, spurred on by the mass media and dreaming of easy money, swarms of investors (both veterans and greenhorns) piled into the stock markets all over the world during the two years (1999–2000) of the "technological boom," just as El Dorado and Klondike gold diggers had done before them. The prices of certain internet-related shares went through the roof. In 1999, a dozen companies saw their share values multiply a hundred-fold. Others, like America OnLine (AOL) did even better: the value of their shares was suddenly 800 times higher than in 1992.

THE NASDAQ CRASH

Anyone with some savings, who had invested as little as €1,000 in the shares of any of the five leading internet companies (AOL, Yahoo!, Amazon, AtHome and eBay) when they first came on to the stock market, would have earned €1 million by April 9, 1999. The Nasdaq index (the exchange where the bulk of high technology stocks are negotiated in New York) showed a gain of 85.6 percent for 1999. This get-rich-quick scenario, with neither work nor effort, tends to be little more than stardust. After March 2000, the Nasdaq began to fall, dragging with it most of the world's technological and telecommunications stocks.

Paradoxically, during the years of the technological boom, the inequality gap continued to widen. When the Nasdaq began to crash in March 2000, it reached proportions not seen since the Great Depression. The prosperity of the "new economy" has turned out to be so fragile that it brings to mind the economic boom of the 1920s, years (like 1999 and 2000) of low inflation and high levels of productivity. With the vertiginous takeoff of the Nasdaq index, some pundits were quick to predict a "technological crash" and announce a "risk of bankruptcy," dire forebodings that saw the specter of 1929 loom once again.[3]

At present, it is estimated that barely 25 percent of companies in the internet economy will be able to survive in the medium term. High-ranking financial authorities had, in fact, warned off investors since the early days. "We should be cautious about shares in internet companies," said Arnout Wellink, president of the Central Bank of Holland, in March 2000. He compared the punters to "mad riders running their horses after each other in the hope of finding a goldmine."[4] People say that political revolutions devour their own children. One might say the same of economic revolutions.

ARGENTINA, A TEXTBOOK CASE

The economic cyclone that broke over Argentina at the end of December 2001 not only caused violent disturbances resulting in 30 deaths, plunging the country into chaos, but it also brought down the government and no less than five presidents in less than two weeks.

This crisis is instructive in more ways than one.[5] Since 1989, Argentina had religiously followed the recommendations of the IMF and other international financial agencies. It privatized the full complement of state assets (oil, mines, electricity, water, telephone, roads, railways, subway, airlines... even the postal service), completely liberalized its overseas trade, did away with exchange controls, and fired state employees or cut the salaries and pensions of tens of thousands in order to reduce the state deficit. It even put the Argentine peso on parity with the dollar (enshrining this in the constitution) so that no future government could devalue it.

Nevertheless, the money raised from the sale of all these state assets, totaling tens of billions of dollars, simply vanished into thin air because of staggering corruption. There was not even enough left to pay the country's foreign debt! Even more astounding is the fact that this debt, which amounted to $8 billion before the wholesale privatization, was more than 16 times greater after the sale of the state assets: it ended up at $132 billion.

Yet Argentina continued to be regarded as the IMF's star pupil. In March 2002, its minister of economy, Domingo Cavallo, the prime mover of privatization and dollarization, was hailed by the *New York Times* as "liberal hero of the year." Argentina thus came to be the example cited by the acolytes of ultraliberalism, who never tired of intoning the praises of the "Argentine model." It was this very model which, after four years of economic recession, tragically fell apart in December 2001.

Elected on the night of January 1, 2002, the Peronist president, Eduardo Duhalde, turned his back on the "neoliberal model" in his investiture speech. "My commitment, from today onward," he announced, "is to discard this obsolete model that has plunged the immense majority of our people into despair." This model, continued Duhalde, "has led to the impoverishment of two million of our compatriots, destroyed the middle class, ruined our industries and reduced the work of the Argentine people to nothing."[6] Rarely had the evils of ultraliberalism been denounced so clearly and in such severe terms.

The catastrophe that so cruelly affected Argentina, as in several Southeast Asian countries in 1997, threatened other countries also, particularly Turkey, Russia, Brazil, South Africa and the Philippines. Even if the markets had anticipated the Argentine crash, the slowing down of the world economy heightened investors' reluctance to run risks and opened up a period of acute economic uncertainty.

GIANT ENTERPRISES, PYGMY STATES

The case of Argentina shows yet again that the globalization of finance capital is pushing peoples around the world into a state of generalized insecurity. It bypasses nations and states, degrading them and their right to exercise democracy and guarantee the common good.

The globalization of finance has created its own state, a supranational state with its own devices, spheres of influence and means of action. It consists of the IMF, the World Bank, the OECD and the WTO. These four institutions speak as one — their unanimous voice boomed out by almost all of the leading branches of the media — to exalt the "virtues of the market." This worldwide state is a power without a society. It permits the finance markets and the macro-companies it governs to form new societies, while at the same time converting true human societies into societies without power.[7] The phenomenon gets worse by the minute.

After taking over from the GATT in 1995, the WTO became an institution with supranational powers, free from the control of any parliamentary democracy. If consulted, the WTO can declare that national legislation on work, the environment and public health is "not in the interests of free trade" and demand that it be repealed.[8]

Not a week goes by without the mass media announcing new mergers and takeovers, some new marriage between big companies, rapprochement between colossi, or a mega-fusion from which new macro-enterprise emerges. We need only recall, for example, the take-over of the car manufacturer Chrysler by Daimler-Benz (for a total of €43 billion); of Citycorp by Travelers (€82.9 million); of the telephone company Ameritech by SBC Communications (€60 million); of the pharmaceutical company Ciba by Sandoz, giving rise to Novartis (€36.3 million); of MCI Communication by WorldCom (€30 million), of the Bank of Tokyo by Mitsubishi Bank (€33.8 million); and of the Société de Banque Suisse by the Union des Banques Suisses (€24.3 million). Then there was the merger agreed between the two historical giants of German iron and steel industry, Thyssen and Krupp, whose turnover, according to its directors, will amount to €63 trillion. The biggest operation in the world, however, has hitherto been the takeover of the cable operator AT&T Broadband by the U.S. telecommunications group Comcast to the tune of €73 billion.

In 1997 alone, takeover and merger operations around the world represented a sum of more than €1.6 trillion. In 2001, despite the general economic recession and the collapse of the technological stock market, the worldwide total from takeovers and mergers rose to €1.958 trillion. The sectors most affected in this race toward gigantism are the banking, pharmaceutical, chemical, media, telecommunications, agricultural and automotive industries.

What is all this excitement about? In the framework of globalization, the big groups in the triad (the United States, the European Union and Japan), making the most of deregulation of the world economy, aim to have a global presence. Their goal is to become the leading actors in all the major countries, cornering the most significant areas of their markets. The lowering of interest rates (which involves a shift of capital from bonds to investment); the huge amounts of capital withdrawn from the stock exchanges of Asia and Latin America (after the Asian crisis of 1997 and the Argentine crash in 2001); the tremendous financial capacity of the main U.S. and British pension funds; and a higher profitability of companies (in Europe and the United States) — combined to reactivate the western stock exchanges in 1999 and 2000, bringing about a veritable rash of mergers.

These mergers face less and less impediments. The automotive industry, once regarded by most governments as a sector as strategic as the iron, steel and telecommunications industries, lost this status about 20 years ago in the United Kingdom. This occurred in the United States after the takeover of Chrysler by the German company Daimler-Benz.

This trend is also confirmed in Germany, the leading economic power in the euro zone, with the decision of Gerhard Schröeder's government to eliminate capital gains tax for companies selling out. In force as of January 1, 2002, this measure was designed to speed up the transformation of German capitalism into Anglo-Saxon capitalism. It favored mergers between companies operating in the same strategic sectors, as was demonstrated in the summer of 2001 with the takeover of the Dresdner Bank by the insurance company Allianz, to the tune of €19.7 billion.

"Nowadays, owners no longer have any inhibitions," stated an expert from the Boston Consulting Group. "The locks and bolts of traditional capitalism have been blown open and mutual pacts of nonaggression are not worth the paper they are written on. It is no longer against the rules to hammer at the door of some group, even if its board of directors is totally against the idea of an approach."[9] In March 1998, France provided an eloquent example with the merger-absorption of Havas by the General Water Company of Jean-Marie Messier, giving rise to the Vivendi group. It subsequently became Vivendi-Universal after being acquired by the U.S. company Universal.

COLOSSAL DIMENSIONS

For predators, mergers offer countless advantages. They make it possible to reduce the effects of competition, bringing together companies that wish to dominate the sector in an almost monopolistic manner.[10] They minimize delays in research and development by absorbing technologically advanced companies. Finally, they enable massive staff reductions under the pretext of cutting costs (in the first year after the merger of the British pharmaceutical companies Glaxo and Wellcome, for example, 7,500 jobs were abolished, meaning that 10 percent of the staff were dismissed).

Some companies have attained mammoth dimensions. In many cases their turnover exceeds the GNPs even of numerous developed countries. For example, General Motors turns over more than the GNP of Denmark, Exxon more than that of Norway and Toyota more than that of Portugal.[11] The total financial resources of these companies frequently exceeds the income of states, even the most developed ones and, above all, the exchange reserves in the central banks of most of the big states.[12] They are like communicating vessels: as the giant companies grow through mergers, states are shrinking as they relinquish their economic assets through privatization.

Since Margaret Thatcher began her privatizing crusade in the early 1980s, everything (or just about everything) has gone up for sale. Everywhere. Most governments, left and right alike, from the rich North or the poor South, don't hesitate before dismantling their state and public service assets. In the 1990s, states all around the world handed over assets for the subsequent benefit of private companies. These assets valued more than €513 billion — €215 billion of which corresponded to the European Union. These privatized companies are especially attractive to investors, as they have previously undergone state-financed restructuring, which, moreover, has also cancelled their debts. These are extraordinarily appealing options, particularly in the services sector (electricity, gas, water, transport, telecommunications, health, etc.), where the state has made substantial earlier investments. These investments should be good for years, guaranteeing that the companies will give regular, profitable, risk-free earnings.

In this situation, we are witnessing the great spectacle of the power of global enterprises, a power which highlights the growing impotence of traditional counterbalancing powers (states, parties and unions). The basic phenomenon of our times, neoliberal globalization, is free of state control, and states continue to lose their former prerogatives to the macro-companies. Powerless citizens are observing a new kind of planetary coup d'état. Simultaneously we can note that social evils that were thought to be eradicated are flourishing once again, in both the developed and underdeveloped worlds, a prime example being the exploitation of children.

SHATTERED CHILDHOODS

There are some signs which cannot be misunderstood. In addition to the reappearance of begging, unemployment, soup kitchens, "dangerous elements" in neighborhoods and dormitory "cities," the figure of the child laborer is yet further proof of the dehumanization that comes hand-in-hand with the economic globalization of this *fin de siècle*.

In the 19th century, burgeoning inequality was particularly reflected in the exploitation of children, as their presence became generalized in the working world. In his famous 1840 report describing the situation of child laborers in France, working 14-hour days, Louis Villermé described "this multitude of children, some of them barely seven years old, dirty, gaunt, dressed in rags, who walk to the factories barefoot in the mud, wan, weak and conveying the image of poverty, suffering and misery incarnate."[13]

Far from being moved by this reality — also denounced by novelists such as Charles Dickens, Victor Hugo, Hector Malot, Jules Vallès, Émile Zola and Edmondo de Amicis — some liberals have considered it a "necessary evil," writing:

> This poverty is a salutary spectacle for the section of the less privileged classes which manages to remain healthy. It is the best way to fill them with terror, urging them on to the difficult virtues they must practise in order to attain a higher status in society.[14]

In the face of such cynicism, how could we fail to understand the indignation of Karl Marx? In his 1848 work, *The Communist Manifesto*, Marx denounced the fact that "by the action of modern industry, all family ties among the proletariat are torn asunder, and their children transformed into simple articles of commerce and instruments of labor." He went on to call for the "abolition of children's factory labor in its present form."[15]

History has shown that the progressive abolition of child labor and the introduction of compulsory education were the indispensable conditions for development in Western Europe and the United States. Nonetheless, it was only in 1990 that the Convention on the Rights of the Child was ratified in the United Nations, although the United States did not sign. It subsequently came into force to fix a minimum age for entry into the labor force, as the International Labor Organization (ILO) had been requesting since 1973.

Even so, it is calculated that there are 200 million child workers around the world, some of them not yet five years old. While many of them may live in the poor and underdeveloped countries, their exploiters are the states of the developed world. There are also more than two million of these children in the European Union as a whole, particularly in the areas most affected by ultraliberal restructuring, like the United Kingdom. The phenomenon of the child worker has also reappeared in "considerably advanced" countries such as Denmark and Holland. "France, too," states an expert from UNICEF (UN International Children's Emergency Fund), "has tens of thousands of child laborers who engage in remunerated work under the guise of apprenticeships. Fifty-nine percent of these so-called apprentices work more than 40 hours per week and, in some cases, up to 60."[16]

SLAVES AND SERFS

The number of child laborers continues to grow around the world. In some countries, like Pakistan, it is a tragedy of immense proportions: tens of millions of children under six years old are victims of this exploitation.[17] In Latin America, one in every five children works; in Africa, one in every three; in Asia, one in two! In agriculture, the sector which employs most children, slavery is enforced as a form of debt collection. Children, with their labor, have to pay the debts accrued by their parents or grandparents. Slaves in every sense of the word, these children will never escape their condition: they are doomed to spend the rest of their lives on the plantation, where they will marry only to bring new slaves into the world.

A great number of children work in the informal economy, in the handicraft industry, small businesses, or begging. Domestic labor (in the Maghreb, the Middle East, West Africa and Latin America) is one of the most detrimental to children, because they are subjected to all kinds of humiliation and violence, especially of a sexual nature. The basic cause of their helplessness is poverty, a poverty exacerbated by advancing economic globalization.

Of the six billion inhabitants of the planet, five billion are victims of poverty. There are more and more associations, forming around the ILO and UNICEF, that are mobilizing in response to this reality, trying to end one of the most appalling scandals of our times and reclaim every child's right to a decent life. Their campaign is primarily aimed at the world's heads of state and governments. They have confirmed that many of these political leaders, not excluding the most powerful among them, are prone to the fever of easy money and speculation; in this era of globalization, they too succumb to corruption.

HOUNDED PRESIDENTS

Almost the whole world over, presidents, occasionally those who are in office following a democratic vote, are being persecuted, prosecuted and harassed without the least regard for their office. Until quite recently, their status was considered almost sacred, making them virtually untouchable. This is no longer the case. Those who talk about "the definitive end of the *ancien régime*" are not entirely off the track because it is, so to speak, the "majesty" of the presidential office that has been decapitated before our very eyes.

Jacques Chirac was reelected in France on May 5, 2002, winning 82.5 percent of the votes to rule out the far-right candidate, Jean-Marie Le Pen. Pursued as he is by the judges and reviled by the media, he is not the only hounded president. The presidents who met in Genoa from July 20 to 22, 2001, at the summit of the world's seven richest countries (the G7 and, with Russia, the G8) faced huge and angry demonstrations. Yet these protests were aimed, not at them personally but at the faceless globalization that they personify. These heads of state and government offer the detestable image of a club of rich, arrogant men, closed off from the world on board a luxury trans-Atlantic liner; sheltered behind militarized walls, safe from the people's rage; protected in a state of war by police who did not hesitate to kill one young protester, Carlo Guiliani, who was 23 years old.

Besieged by some 200,000 demonstrators and clearly upset, the G7 presidents limited themselves to repeating a single mantra in their own defense — "We have been democratically elected!" — as if this were some magic charm. As if they were telling us something new! Being democratically elected in no way authorizes any president to betray his or her electoral promises or the public interest, or to go privatizing and liberalizing left, right and center. Nor does it entitle them to fulfill the demands of the companies that finance their electoral campaigns regardless of the social cost. At least two of the seven — George W. Bush and Silvio Berlusconi — are representatives of the financial circles in their countries rather than the citizens.

Nowadays, the harassment of rulers particularly affects those heads of state or government accused of war crimes or crimes against humanity. General Augusto Pinochet, the former dictator of Chile, was detained in London in 1998 at the request of the Spanish Judge Baltasar Garzón. He was returned to Chile in March 2000, to be charged once again by the Chilean Judge Juan Guzmán. The legal action taken against him was definitively suspended on June 9, 2001, supposedly because of the "deterioration in the state of mental health of the former dictator."

MORAL DEMANDS

The Pinochet case caused a radical acceleration in the struggle against the impunity enjoyed by political leaders on the international stage. Since then, we have seen more than one political leader hauled before the judges. One was General Nezzar from Algeria, accused by a Paris judge of "war crimes" committed in his country during the dirty war against the Islamic fundamentalists. Another was the former U.S. secretary of state, Henry Kissinger, called before an examining magistrate in Paris for his alleged involvement in the 1973 coup d'état against Salvador Allende, the socialist president of Chile. The Israeli prime minister, Ariel Sharon, has been obliged to steer clear of Belgium, where he is accused of complicity in the Sabra and

Chatila massacres perpetrated in Beirut in 1982.

Similarly, charges of "complicity in acts of torture" were made against the former president of Chad, Hissène Habré. On February 3, 2000, he was placed under house arrest in Senegal where he had taken refuge. More recently we saw the case of Argentine General Jorge Videla who became president after his 1976 coup d'état. On July 10, 2001, he was accused and put into preventive detention for his alleged participation in Operation Condor, the death pact established between Latin American dictatorships and the CIA in the 1970s to systematically "disappear" those who opposed them. And, on June 29, 2001, we witnessed the controversial appearance of the former president of Yugoslavia, Slobodan Milosevic, before the International Criminal Court for the former Yugoslavia (ICCY) in The Hague to answer for "crimes against humanity."

Yet, perpetrators of violent crimes are not the only ones who are persecuted and prosecuted. Nowadays, democratically elected presidents are obliged to answer to the courts, mainly on charges of corruption. Here too, moral requirements are manifested on the international stage. Before being definitively acquitted, Argentine President Carlos Menem was detained in June 2001, and put under house arrest facing accusations of illegal arms sales and collecting secret commissions to the tune of several million dollars during his mandates (1989–99). His former neoliberal accomplice and minister of economy, Domingo Cavallo, the man who brought in peso-dollar parity and privatized industry on a huge scale, was also subsequently detained.

Also a democratically elected representative, Alberto Fujimori, the former president of Peru, took refuge in Japan in November 2000, fleeing justice after he had been accused of corruption and murder. Vladimiro Montesinos, his former right-hand man and regime strongman, was detained in July 2001. In the Philippines, mass pressure forced President Joseph Estrada to step down on January 20, 2001, because of a corruption-related scandal. Estrada was detained on April 25, 2001, and accused of misappropriating €80 million from public funds. In Indonesia, President Wahid was dismissed on July 23, 2001, accused of corruption. On December 28, 2001, the former president of Congo-Brazzaville, Pascal Lissouba, was tried in absencia and condemned to 30 years' hard labor for high treason and misappropriation of oil-for-aid funds. There is no shortage of examples we might cite.

The persecution of political leaders is not exclusive to the democratic and developed countries of the rich North. As may be seen, it extends to numerous countries of the developing world, as if financial globalization has brought with it a corresponding globalization in moral exigency. The phenomenon is spreading almost as fast as the antiglobalization movement: in the period between Seattle and Genoa, less than two years, the movement has gone from a picturesque and isolated form of protest and become the revolt of a generation, a planetary social war.

For these protesters, disarming the financial powers must become a priority civic goal if the world of the 21st century is not to be ruled by the law of the jungle.

Speculation on movements in the currency market shifts about €1.6 trillion every day. The instability of prices is one of the causes of the rise in real interest rates, which acts as a brake on domestic consumption and business investment. It increases public deficits, and stimulates pension funds (that move hundreds of billions of euros) to demand ever-greater dividends from business. The first victims in this "race" for profits are the wage earners, whose dismissal in huge numbers — termed "stock market convenience sackings" — multiplies the value of their former employers' shares on the stock exchange.

Can democratic societies indefinitely tolerate the intolerable? It is imperative that these devastating movements of capital are restricted. There are three ways of doing so: eliminating "tax havens," increasing capital gains taxes and taxing finance speculation and transactions.

Tax havens are simply places where banking secrecy is the order of the day; their function is to cover up misappropriations and other criminal activities. Thanks to their intermediary activities, billions of dollars bypass the tax system, only benefiting the already powerful and the finance establishments. All of the world's great banks have branches in tax havens, where they glean their most succulent profits. Why not decree a financial boycott, for example, on Gibraltar, the Cayman Islands, Monaco and Liechtenstein, and prohibit banks that work with public institutions from establishing branches in their territories?

The imposition of capital gains taxes is a minimum democratic requirement. They should be imposed in the same way as income tax, but this happens nowhere, not even in the European Union.

The total freedom of the circulation of capital destabilizes democracy. Deterrent mechanisms must be created to remedy this. One such mechanism is the Tobin Tax, named in honor of the Nobel Economics Prize laureate, James Tobin, who proposed it as early as 1972. The idea is to tax, in a reasonable fashion, all stock market transactions. It would act as a stabilizing measure, while at the same time obtaining income for the international community. At a rate of 0.1 percent, the Tobin Tax would produce an amount of €166 trillion per year, double the annual amount needed to eradicate extreme poverty within five years.[18]

Numerous experts have demonstrated that there would be no technical difficulties in introducing this tax.[19] Applying it would put paid to the neoliberal credo of those who proclaim that there is no way the present system can be changed.

In April 1998, the NGO Action for a Taxation of Financial Transactions to Aid Citizens (ATTAC) was created in Paris, with the eventual aim of establishing branches throughout the world. At the time of writing it has some 40,000 members in France. Working in conjunction with unions and cultural, social and ecological associations, ATTAC acts as a formidable civic pressure group, encouraging parliaments and governments to call for the definitive introduction of this worldwide tax in solidarity.

ATTAC is also concerned with mass education. Along with other organizations, it holds seminars offering a critical analysis of the finance economy around the world. In this regard, ATTAC was an instigator of one of the most audacious projects to form part of the intellectual and social response to globalization: the World Social Forum of Porto Alegre.

PORTO ALEGRE

The 21st century began with Porto Alegre. People from around the world who oppose or criticize neoliberal globalization met between January 25 and 30, 2001, and from January 31 to February 5, 2002, in the south of Brazil, with Porto Alegre as the headquarters of the first World Social Forums.[20] In 2004, the WSF will take place in Mumbai, India.

This was not, as in Seattle, Quebec, Genoa and other places, to protest against the global injustices, inequalities and disasters caused by the excesses of neoliberalism. In a positive and constructive spirit, the aim of Porto Alegre was to propose a theoretical and practical framework for a different kind of globalization, and to affirm that another world is possible, less inhuman and more caring.

This kind of Rebel International[21] met in Porto Alegre at the same time as the World Economic Forum (WEF) was being held in Davos (Switzerland) in 2001, in New York in 2002, and in Davos in 2003. For some decades, the WEF has brought together the new rulers of the world and, in particular, the directors of globalization. These leaders can no longer hide their concern about this phenomenon of resistance, and are taking very seriously the demonstrations that have systematically been held to coincide with every summit of the world's de facto rulers: the WTO, the IMF, the World Bank, the OECD, the G7 and the European Union.

The events of Seattle[22] made a deep impression on the leaders who met in Davos in 1999. As one journalist noted, there is always one star of the WEF. In 2000, there was no doubt about it: the star of Davos was Seattle. More than any other topic, it was Seattle they were talking about.[23] Aware of the democratic deficit inherent in globalization, some supporters of the present dominant model have begun to call for serious reflection, particularly regarding the modification of the rules and processes of globalization to make it more democratic.[24] Even Alan Greenspan, chairman of the U.S. Federal Reserve, has gone so far as to state, "Societies cannot prosper when there are significant sectors that perceive their functioning as unjust."[25]

Coming from the four corners of the Earth, these "significant sectors" are opposed to the present-day economic barbarism and do not accept that neoliberalism is an "insurmountable horizon." In Porto Alegre, they have attempted to lay the foundations for a true countervailing power,[26] with an enthusiasm that might be described as revolutionary.

DREAMERS OF THE ABSOLUTE

Why in Porto Alegre of all places? For some years now Porto Alegre has been an emblematic city. Capital of the southern-most state in Brazil, Rio Grande do Sul, and near the border of Uruguay, Porto Alegre is something of a social laboratory that has fascinated international observers.[27]

Governed in an unique fashion for the past 13 years by a left-wing coalition headed by the Brazilian Workers' Party (PT), the city has developed spectacularly in many areas: housing, public transport, roads, garbage collection, community clinics, hospitals, sewerage drains, literacy, schooling, culture, safety, etc. And the secret of this success? A participative budget (*orçamento participativo*), which means that the residents of the various neighborhoods can decide very specifically and democratically how municipal funds are to be used. In short, they decide what kinds of infrastructure they want to create or improve and then follow, step by step, the progress of the work and compliance with the financial commitments that are made. This makes the misappropriation of funds and other abuses practically impossible, as the investments made are an exact expression of the wishes of the majority of residents in each neighborhood.

It should be stressed that this political experience, while carried out in total democratic freedom, also faces strong opposition from the right. The PT does not control the major local newspapers, the radio or the television. These are in the hands of influential groups who are allied with local business and hostile to the PT. Obliged as it is to respect the federal constitution of Brazil, the PT has little space to maneuver in terms of political autonomy, especially when it comes to taxation matters. In spite of all this, the satisfaction of the citizens was such that the PT candidate was reelected as lord mayor with more than 63 percent of the votes in October 2002.

In this remarkable city where a democracy unlike any other is flourishing, the WSF was held with the aim of launching a form of globalization that does not exclude the poor. For the last 10 years, capital and the market have reiterated that, contrary to what socialists say, it is they and not the people who write history and create well-being.

In Porto Alegre, some new dreamers of the absolute have reminded us that the economy is not the only thing that can be global: protection of the environment, struggle against inequality and respect for human rights can also be worldwide endeavors. It is up to the world's citizens to accept the challenge once and for all.

THE KOSOVO WAR AND THE NEW WORLD ORDER 5

In March 1999, for the first time since it was created in 1949, NATO went to war with a country which had not committed any act of aggression beyond its own borders — the Federal Republic of Yugoslavia. It was the first time since 1945 that European forces bombed another sovereign state. The decision to do so was described as a "moral duty" by Javier Solana, who was then the secretary general of NATO.

Right from the start of the bombing attacks, NATO forces displayed an improvisation as astounding as it was alarming. The Kosovo War had been embarked upon prematurely and with a lack of preparation that might be described as absolute. What were the supposed aims of this war at the start of the crisis? There were essentially two: reestablishing substantial autonomy for Kosovo (which had been totally stripped of this in 1989), and obliging Belgrade to respect the basic freedoms (political, cultural, religious, linguistic, etc.) of the Kosovars. Achieving these two goals peacefully was the prime objective of the Rambouillet Conference, held from January to March 1999.

Yet the parties concerned, Serbs and Kosovars — the latter represented by the Kosovo Liberation Army (UÇK) — had already reached
agreement on these two basic points.

Slobodan Milosevic's regime had explicitly agreed to concede
wide-ranging autonomy to Kosovo: after the holding of free elections,
the province would have an autonomous government, a legislative
assembly, a president, a judiciary and its own law and order forces.[1]
If both parties had already reached agreement on the essential issues,
why was the Rambouillet Conference a failure? There is only one
reason: the obstinacy of the western powers, above all the United
States, in insisting on the presence of NATO forces in Kosovan territory, and in Yugoslavia as a whole, to supervise the proper application of the agreement, knowing perfectly well that Belgrade would
oppose this presence. This highly predictable opposition was regarded as a casus belli. Belgrade did not oppose the use of other European
troops (from the East or West) or, for example, the UN Blue Helmets.

But no, it had to be NATO or war. And war it was.

AN OVER-HASTY DISMANTLING

The peoples of the Balkans are still paying for the obtuseness of the
European Union and the West in general when they turned a blind
eye to the premature dismantling of the former Yugoslavia by the
nationalists. How could such a blunder, described by Richard
Holbrooke as "the greatest collective error of the West, in terms of
security, since the 1930s,"[2] have occurred? The error cost the lives of
more than 100,000 people, and it was avoidable.[3]

Former resistance leader Josip Broz Tito reunified the peoples of
Yugoslavia after 1945 in spite of the atrocities committed during the
war, especially by Croatian Ustasha and Serbian Chetniks. The
nationalists evaporated. Demonstrating that the thesis of "ancestral
hatred" was absurd, Tito supported cohesion. As he liked to say,
Yugoslavia had six republics, five nations, four languages, three
religions, two alphabets and only one party.

After his death in 1980, the leadership of the Communist Party that had once stood up to the Soviet Union and had constructed the land of "workers' self-management," began to falter. The principle of an annual presidency rotating between the six republics resulted in a weakening of the federation. Added to this was the foreign debt crisis which, over a decade, caused thousands of strikes and created enormous tension between the rich areas of the federal republic (Slovenia and Croatia) and the rest.

This discord, stoked by the mass media, ushered in a resurgence of nationalist bigotry. In his memoirs, a former U.S. ambassador to Belgrade recalls that the television propagated an inter-ethnic hatred that spread through Yugoslavia like an epidemic. Media images encouraged a whole generation of Serbs, Bosnians and Muslims to hate their neighbors.[4] Another eyewitness describes how watching the television in Belgrade he could see how the Bosnian Serbs came to believe that they would become the victims of the Ustasha forces or fundamentalist Muslims: it was just as if U.S. television had come under the control of the Ku Klux Klan.[5]

In 1989, on the sixth centenary of the Turkish defeat of the Serbs, on the ground where the Battle of Merles had taken place, Slobodan Milosevic gave an outrageously virulent speech to one million people, stirring up the new and revitalized wave of nationalist hatred. Other leaders — Franjo Tudjman in Croatia and Alija Izetbegovic in Bosnia — responded with tirades that were no less extreme.

The countries of the West, still in shock from the fall of the Berlin Wall, the death throes of the Soviet Union and military victory in the Gulf War, were unable to prevent disaster. In their haste to recognize the independence of Slovenia and Croatia, Germany and the Vatican even accelerated the process.

The Slovenia War broke out on June 27, 1991, with the wars of Croatia and Bosnia and their respective criminal outrages hot on its heels. The European Union only revealed its inexperience and ineptitude when it used the occasion to assert that it could impose, within the continent and by force if necessary, a just and equitable solution for everyone. With the Dayton Peace Agreements of 1995, the United

States reestablished a peace that was all too precarious, as subsequent events would prove.

A POOR AND OVERPOPULATED REGION

Inhabited by Albanians (non-Slavic and mainly Muslim), 90 percent of Kosovo is poor: it has the highest underemployment and illiteracy figures in Europe. It is overpopulated, with two million inhabitants in 10,900 square kilometers, and has a birthrate of 40 percent, while more than half of the population is under 20 years of age. Given its distinctive cultural characteristics, Kosovo has clamored since time immemorial for a law giving it fully operational republican status within the Federation of Yugoslavia. The 1947 Constitution only conceded it status as a province of Serbia, although with considerable autonomy, meaning it was a de facto semi-republic with the right to vote.

The abolition of this law in 1989 brought with it, *inter alia*, the dissolution of the Kosovan Parliament, the prohibition of teaching in Albanian in schools, the sacking of more than a 150,000 Albanian speakers from the public service and public companies and the introduction of martial law giving unlimited powers to Belgrade's repressive forces. These forces intensified their work of proliferating the humiliation and brutality already endured by the Kosovan Albanians for more than a decade, in order to push them to emigrate. Together, all of these circumstances could only lead to revolt.

The resistance, passive among the supporters of Ibrahim Rugova, became increasingly violent among UÇK militants who, in 1997 and 1998, stepped up their deadly attacks against the law and order forces of Yugoslavia and the Serbian minority. Blown out of all proportion by the Serbian mass media, these attacks provided just the pretext sought by the propaganda apparatus of Slobodan Milosevic's regime to inflame the Serbian crowds. They played the nationalist card ("Kosovo, cradle of the Serbian nation," "holy territory," "land of our ancestors," "Serbs: victims," etc.) and successfully whipped up anti-Albanian racism.

Prior to the 1999 war, the confrontations in Kosovo had led to the deaths of some 2,000 Kosovars, with the destruction of 300 villages, while more than 200,000 refugees had left their homes. In October 1998, with the threat of a NATO intervention, Slobodan Milosevic signed an agreement whereby he would withdraw his army and authorize the OSCE (Organization for Security and Cooperation in Europe) to station some 1,600 unarmed observers from the Kosovo Verification Mission (KVM) in the zone.

The European Union, in order not to encourage the fragmentation of Europe into microstates, and to prevent the conflict from spreading throughout the entire region (the nearest focus being Macedonia, with Albanians comprising 30 percent of its population), declined to support independence for Kosovo. Instead, it proposed that an agreement should be signed in order to concede the maximum possible autonomy to the province.

A CASCADE OF CONSEQUENCES

It is not difficult to see that this was a highly complex situation, like all geopolitical issues in the Balkans. The quest for compromise was a delicate and arduous business. Accordingly, the negotiations of the Rambouillet Conference (January–March 1999) should have been prolonged for some weeks more, especially in view of the fact that the presence of several thousand OSCE observers in Kosovo partially protected the Kosovars from further violence.

History teaches that, in this volatile region, any untimely political action triggers a cascade of unintended consequences. This was tragically confirmed in 1989, when Slobodan Milosevic unilaterally abolished the autonomous status of Kosovo and Voivodina, and in 1991, when Germany and the Vatican too hastily recognized Slovenia's independence. The NATO air attacks launched at the end of March 1999 only proved it yet again.

Aimed in principle at destroying the repressive machinery of Milosevic's regime, the bombing attacks were immediately and predictably answered with reprisals against the Kosovan Albanians by the Belgrade authorities. It is difficult to understand the myopia of NATO's leaders who, with their initiative, thrust the Kosovars into a situation of risk comparable only to that in which the Turkish Armenians were placed during the Russian offensive of 1915. The latter, regarded by the Turkish authorities as a "potential fifth column," were, as is now well known, victims of the first genocide of the 20th century.

NATO, tirelessly presenting Milosevic as a dictator, could not have been ignorant of the fact that the Serbs had plans for sweeping ethnic cleansing operations in Kosovo, or that Milosevic's ultranationalist allies were desperate to put them into practise.

The bombings, however, had other, unforeseen victims. Since the decision to go ahead was made without the express authorization of the UN Security Council, the bombings had the effect of further discrediting the United Nations. In most of the countries involved, the decision was authorized by the executive, without consultation or voting that might have meant representation at the national level, thereby undermining the national parliaments. On the ground, the bombing attacks were, regardless, a harsh blow against Serbian (and sometimes Kosovan) civilians, who were victims of numerous targeting errors, while the destruction of factories and economic infrastructure led to hundreds of thousands of people being left without work. The daily lives of ordinary citizens were gradually reduced to a living hell.

Contrary to what was apparently expected, the bombings did not encourage the people to detest Slobodan Milosevic. Rather, the sense of being the victims of a collective punishment reinforced a feeling of national unity among the Serbs, and they rallied around their government. In this atmosphere, with feelings running high and "our land in danger," NATO's "victims" obliged Serbian democrats who were hostile to the regime to respond as patriots, and to cease all anti-Milosevic criticism.

As if this were not enough, the Chinese Embassy in Belgrade was bombed by NATO forces. The Chinese (China being a permanent member of the UN Security Council) became even more hostile toward NATO's policy. At the diplomatic level, Russia, inevitably an actor on the Balkans scene for the last two centuries, was also humiliated.

THE "ZERO CASUALTIES" PRINCIPLE

The way the Balkans conflict was run also constituted a new type of war. In all of military history, never has a conflict been managed in the way that General Wesley Clark, supreme allied commander of NATO, managed this one. The principle of "zero casualties" became an absolute imperative. After two months of bombing, not a single soldier from the alliance had died in action. This was unprecedented.

Material damage for the attackers was also insignificant. Although more than 25,000 air missions were flown, only two planes were lost (whose pilots were found safe and sound on enemy soil by infiltrated commandos), in keeping with General Clark's project to fight a "war without loss of aircraft."[6] Not a single boat, tank or helicopter was put out of action in the course of operations.

In contrast, the damage inflicted on Yugoslavia was considerable. Military and industrial installations (power stations included) were seriously damaged or rendered completely useless, as was the main transport infrastructure (bridges, railways and roads). The allies jammed electronic systems and kept permanent taps on the telephone lines. Even though, as was discovered later, the Serbian Army managed to "go to ground" quite effectively, and successfully used ingenious "decoys," several thousand Yugoslav military personnel died in the bombing attacks. According to some U.S. generals, the bombing set the country back two decades.

The disparity of military strength between NATO and Yugoslavia was so great that it is hardly appropriate to talk of a war. Rather, it was a punitive action. It was punishment of a type no country has ever suffered before, apart from Iraq (in both gulf wars!) and, after September 11, 2001, Afghanistan. The NATO strategy forced the Yugoslavs into an impotent passivity before the Allied forces, which remained beyond their reach throughout.

We should really, however, be talking about two wars. One is that of the strong against the weak, or NATO against Yugoslavia, which, as we have noted, was a punitive strike. The other is that of the weak party against the weaker party, of Serbia against the Kosovars, the forces of Belgrade against the UÇK. One is the ultramodern, high-tech, electronic war, and the other is characterized by massacres committed with two-handled saws, massive deportations and summary executions.

There is another novel feature of this conflict: NATO explicitly declared that it did not want fatalities, not of the Serbian military and still of less civilians. It was to be a war of apparatus against apparatus, machine against machine — almost a videogame. When civilians died due to miscalculation, the alliance bent over backwards with excuses, lamentations, remorse, breast-beating and other pleas for forgiveness.

Crushing an abstract enemy, yes; killing a specific enemy, no. "In neowar," notes Umberto Eco, "he who has killed excessively is the loser for public opinion."[7] Such was the new set of rules imposed by this war and the mass media attentively ensured that they were respected. Needless to say, manipulating the latter became one of the prime objectives of the warring parties.

DEMOCRATIC CENSORSHIP AND AFFABLE PROPAGANDA

In this respect, the Kosovo War contributed nothing essentially new with regard to the "Malvinas" model,[8] established in 1982 and successfully applied in 1991 during the Gulf War. In all the essential aspects, NATO set up a media device in Kosovo that had been dreamed up in 1986 and refined after lessons learned in the Gulf War. In brief, the aim was to make the war invisible, while NATO would become the main source of information for journalists. The journalists, while undoubtedly more discerning, could not always avoid this new form of "democratic censorship and affable propaganda," all the more so when the traditional censorship and out-

and-out propaganda of Belgrade did nothing to produce any revelations approaching the truth.

The media, then, were reduced in these two months to commenting on a crucial absent image: atrocities committed by Belgrade's forces against the civilian population of Kosovo. Eyewitness reports of many deportees described crimes whose reality was unquestionable,[9] but we were shown no images to demonstrate them, and not a single reporter saw them with his or her own eyes. This constitutes a failure for the media machine, particularly the audiovisual branch of it, which has spent the past 10 years trying to convince us that reporting essentially consists of allowing us to "witness the event."

This, too, gave rise to polemic. The defenders of NATO's "official version," and some dissident and iconoclastic observers, were at loggerheads. In the United Kingdom, for example, the foreign minister, Robin Cook, publicly attacked John Simpson, a BBC correspondent in Belgrade, accusing him of being an accomplice of Milosevic. Simpson had drawn attention to the existence in Serbia of democratic opposition to the regime, and to schools that were destroyed by NATO bombing attacks. The British (Labor) Government went so far as to put pressure on the BBC and demand that the journalist be repatriated. The BBC refused to comply.

In Italy, an RAI correspondent, Ennio Remondino, who harshly criticized the bombing of Belgrade and, in particular, the destruction of the Serbian television building (which killed several staff members), was the object of fierce attacks from journalists and intellectuals who considered him a "Milosevic agent." In France, opinions expressed by the intellectual Régis Debray on his return from a brief visit to Kosovo earned him a veritable media lynching, because they did not coincide with the official version.[10]

MORAL AND HUMANITARIAN REASONS

All in all, this first NATO war could not have been more catastrophic.[11] If this were not enough, the instability it was supposed to quell threatens to become even more widespread. In 2001, it spread to

Macedonia. Tomorrow it could affect Hungary, Bulgaria, Romania and even Greece, Moldavia and Turkey. These countries are, so to speak, in the front line and their governments and populations alike (about 150 million people) are following the latter-day Balkans wars with a mixture of fear and hair-trigger inflammability.

With such a disaster, one can't help but wonder why there was so much hurry about this war. By way of justification, Javier Solana declared, "We must prevent an authoritarian regime from continuing to suppress its people in Europe."[12] Other NATO top brass claimed it was for "moral reasons." Certain commentators said it was for "humanitarian reasons." These are all respectable and certainly legitimate arguments, but they are not sufficient to be convincing in any conclusive way.

There have been and still are other "moral" and "humanitarian" occasions for intervention. For example, the Ankara authorities in Kurdistan have been waging war against the Kurdish population since 1984. The Kurds have been denied the right to autonomy and even to teach in their own language. The toll, so far, of this ongoing war has been the deaths of about 29,000 people and the flight of over one million refugees.[13]

And are there not "moral" and "humanitarian" reasons for offering reparation to the Greek Cypriots for the injustice committed against them in 1974? Victims of an implacable ethnic cleansing, more than 160,000 were expelled from the north of Cyprus in the cruelest of circumstances. This followed the invasion by the Turkish Army, which continues its illegal occupation of this half of the island where it has encouraged the arrival of more than 60,000 settlers from Turkey.

Finally, are there not "moral" and "humanitarian" reasons to intervene on behalf of the hundreds of thousands of Palestinians who have been subjected to all kinds of repression, whose land has been taken, and who have been expelled from their territory by Israeli authorities that persist in emptying East Jerusalem of its Palestinian population while also urging Jewish colonization of the West Bank and Gaza, in flagrant contempt of international agreements and UN resolutions?

Are the situations of these three communities — Kurds, Greek Cypriots and Palestinians — any less horrific than that of the Kosovan Albanians? Why does the West favor negotiation in some places (and rightly so) and opt for bombing in others? The reasons are political, not moral. Turkey and Israel are democratic states with market economies, and are old military allies of the West. They are also a long way from the heartland of the European Union.

STRATEGIC SIGNIFICANCE

Kosovo is another kettle of fish. The European Union and the United States had their own particular and urgent reasons for intervention. Strategic reasons motivated the European Union. The strategic significance of the region, however, is no longer what it was. In days of old, a zone was "strategically significant" when its conquest and possession offered considerable military advantages (access to the sea, navigable rivers, a crucial elevation, etc.); when there were vital resources to be exploited (oil, gas, coal, iron, water, etc.); and when essential trade routes could be controlled (straits, canals, mountain passes, etc.).

In our times of globalization, the hegemony of finance capital and the "new economy" based on information technology, this concept of "strategic significance" is no longer a major concern. At any rate, Kosovo is not of the least interest from this "strategic" point of view. Taking Kosovo offers the conquering power no military advantage, major resources, or control of any vital trade route.

So, what now determines the strategic significance of a territory for an entity as rich as the European Union? The key issue is a territory's capacity for exporting conflict and chaos: political chaos, chronic poverty, illegal emigration, criminal networks, terrorism, delinquency, drug mafia and prostitution, etc. From this point of view, after the fall of the Berlin Wall, there are two regions that are of high strategic significance for Europe: the Maghreb and the Balkans.

"REALPOLITIK"

The Kosovo crisis heated up definitively after the implosion of Albania in 1997, when the country collapsed into chaos and disorder. This indirectly offered the UÇK combatants the chance to obtain thousands of weapons at bargain prices and to establish a secure rearguard base, a sanctuary from which to launch violent incursions into Kosovo.

This so-called freedom fight, over a territory to which fanatical claims were laid from both sides for the same historical, religious and cultural reasons, by adversaries who were determined to take the conflict through to the bitter end, threatened to be long and cruel. Could the European Union spend the next five or six years with such a situation on its doorstep, with all the predictable repercussions in Macedonia and the rest of the Balkans? Or with tens of thousands of refugees attempting to enter Italy and the rest of the European Union? The answer to these questions has very little to do with moral and humanitarian considerations and a great deal to do with realpolitik, in that it is based on the need to defend the higher interests of states. It therefore took the form of the war and the bombing attacks of the summer of 1999.

Kosovo was of no strategic interest for the United States, in neither the old nor the new sense of the term. For the United States, which had unwillingly become involved in the Balkans crisis in 1991, the Kosovo conflict was now the perfect pretext for sorting out an urgent matter: the new legitimacy of NATO. This defense organization, established in the Cold War period, was conceived as a way of responding to the threat of a specific adversary: the Soviet Union.

With the disappearance of the Soviet Union in December 1991, the collapse of the communist countries and the dissolution of the Warsaw Pact, NATO should also have been dismantled to be replaced in Western Europe by an autochthonous defense organization, the embryo of which was the French-German Brigade, or so we were told.

Washington, however, wants to maintain its status as a European power. It has therefore done everything possible to reinforce NATO and extend its influence, by taking in three countries from the former Eastern Bloc (Poland, the Czech Republic and Hungary). U.S. analyst William Pfaff is quite clear about the fact that NATO has undoubtedly been maintained because of the political influence it gives the United States in Europe, and because it blocks the development of a European strategic system that might constitute a rival for the United States.[14]

That is not all. In the era of neoliberal globalization, the United States wants to transform NATO into the military wing and the security apparatus of this globalization, in order to reinforce its logic and to cut its risks, with the United Kingdom, Germany and France as its main allies among the remaining NATO countries (with the hope of including Japan and South Korea in a second phase). As a result, the United Nations has been thrust aside and diminished to a kind of moral reference point (rather like the Council of Europe with regard to the European Union, or some kind of lay Vatican), with no capacity to intervene in case of crisis.

High-level U.S. officials, however, are now wondering if it might not have been more efficient after all to intervene under a UN mandate, as for example in the Gulf War, rather than under NATO auspices, with all the complications that were posed by permanent consultation with 19 governments.[15] It would have been even easier for the United States to act unilaterally. Its military supremacy enables it to impose a New World Order through its market empire. Is that so extraordinary? Of course not, says Admiral William Perry, secretary of defense of the Clinton Administration: "Since the United States is the only country with global interests, it is also the natural leader of the international community."[16]

Kosovo offered the United States the opportunity to apply NATO's "new strategic concept" just weeks before its official adoption in Washington on April 26, 1999: to extend and reinforce the community of democratic nations. Needless to say, this extension of democracy has as its essential condition the obligatory adoption of the western model of neoliberal globalization, hand-in-hand with submission to the hegemony of the United States. These were the real reasons behind the U.S. participation in the Kosovo War.

CHECHNYA

Since there are certain features that are tragically common to the situations of Kosovo and Chechnya — nationalism, ethnic hatred, the confrontation between radical Islam and orthodox Christianity, secessionism, decolonization and the independence movements, the Kosovo War tends to be compared with the new war the Russian generals began to wage in Chechnya in September 1999.

They are, in fact, two very different cases, though both wars have been particularly inhumane. As in Kosovo after the NATO bombing attacks began, more than two thirds of the population of Chechnya — about 200,000 people — had to flee from the fighting to seek precarious refuge in nearby Ingushia. According to international humanitarian organizations (which were denied permission by the Russian authorities to go anywhere near the front), hundreds of civilians lost their lives in indiscriminate bombing attacks by the Russian Army, an army which also pillaged, raped and committed other war crimes in various towns.

Devastated by the earlier conflict of 1994–96 with its toll of more than 80,000 deaths, Chechnya was once again a terrified witness to the systematic destruction of its main infrastructure. Four years later, the war against the Chechnyan resistance has no end in sight and this small Caucasian republic is at risk of being set back, in terms of its development, to the beginning of the 20th century.

How did a human, economic and ecological disaster of such horrific dimensions occur? How is it possible that the international community, so prompt in 1999 to invoke the right to intervene and to mobilize in favor of Kosovo, could impassively watch a tragedy like this unfold? The main responsibility is certainly Moscow's. When the Soviet Union was being dismantled, it was unable to propose a law of autonomy, based on truly democratic principles, to the entities that remained as part of the Russian Federation. With the complicity of the West, which pushed Moscow to adopt the neoliberal economic model as fast as possible, the Kremlin improvised a form of à la carte federalism and, in exchange for political support, permitted the establishment in each region of "a kind of generalized franchising"[17] of the most lucrative sectors (oil, currency, alcohol, tobacco, caviar, drugs, arms, etc.) to the local clans or the mafia.

This set of circumstances only exacerbated social tensions, particularly in Chechnya. As a region that had provided 40 percent of the Soviet Union's petroleum until 1940, its production of fossil fuels is now down to barely one percent of the Russian total. As its economy went into total freefall, poverty has spread rapidly throughout its territory.

With the rise of the mafia groups there was also a renewed outbreak of nationalist feeling and a resurgence of Sunni Islam, both latent in a country that had resisted Moscow's colonial expansion for more than a century, becoming, in 1859, the last part of the Caucasian bastion to surrender to the Russians. The dispossessed of Chechnya were particularly susceptible to the discourse of Wahabi missionaries who came from Saudi Arabia with abundant financial resources, preaching a traditionalist form of Islam. The Wahabi had already seduced part of the Afghan resistance that had defeated the Soviet Union in the 1980s. Chechnya's leading independence fighters in the early 1990s, including the famous Shamil Basaev, belonged to this Islamic denomination. After the attacks of September 11, 2001, the mass media hastened to link Chechnya with Afghanistan and insistently pointed out that numerous Chechnyans, protégées of the Taliban, were training in al-Qaida camps under the leadership of Osama Bin Laden.

After its unexpected military victory over Moscow in 1996, the holy Chechnyan union began to weaken. Debilitated by the territorial blockade imposed by the Russian forces, the government of Aslan Maskhadov lacked the means to reconstruct the country. The Wahabis set up Islamic fiefdoms in which they imposed Koranic (*Sharia*) law against the will of numerous citizens. In the chaos, mafia gangs and banditry prospered. The country had to endure the development of an economy based on plunder and spoliation: the pillaging of isolated farms, contraband dealing in all kinds of products, the kidnapping of hundreds of people for ransom, many of them foreigners. Largely due to external causes, Chechnya slowly became a chaotic and ungovernable entity, feared by its neighbors and from which its own inhabitants began to flee. In this context of utter corruption, four determining factors set off the present-day conflict.

TERRORIST ATTACKS

For a start, the reopening, in May 1999, of the oil pipeline joining the cities of Baku (Azerbaijan) and Supsa (Georgia), on the shores of the Black Sea, caused considerable unease in Russia. Still more unsettling was the fact that, only months later, Turkey, Azerbaijan and Georgia signed an agreement to construct another pipeline between Baku and the Turkish port of Ceyhan on the Mediterranean, definitively bypassing Russian territory. Moscow felt this as a geopolitical humiliation, and the harbinger of a serious decline of its influence in the Caucasus. This feeling was only exacerbated when the new pipelines came automatically under the protection of the NATO security system.

Next, in August 1999, the incursion into Dagestan by the Chechnyan Islamic leader Basaev confirmed in Russian eyes the danger of contagion entailed in the example of Chechnya's possible independence. This incursion, though swiftly confined and put down, upset Moscow deeply, and threats against its control over such a strategic region as the North Caucasus were seen to be proliferating.

Finally, at the beginning of autumn in 1999, a series of horrific explosives attacks on housing blocks in Russia killed 300 among the civilian population in a number of cities and towns. Although there was no conclusive proof as to who had perpetrated the attacks, the Russian authorities lost no time in blaming the "Chechnyan bandits," inflaming the feelings of a population that had for a decade been sinking further and further into catastrophic social decline.

Evidence of this is the fact that Vladimir Putin used the occasion to declare his "ruthless war against terrorism" and to impose himself as the strong man the Russians had been waiting for. This political dimension, however, is inseparable from the strategic considerations of the war, which, for Moscow, meant preserving its iron grip on Chechnya while also reestablishing Russia as the dominant power throughout the Caucasus. This amounted to nothing more than a simple regional ambition for what was once a world superpower.

NEW WORLD ORDER

In contrast, the war between NATO and the former Federal Republic of Yugoslavia opened up in the spring of 1999 a new phase in international relations and announced nothing less than the dawn of a New World Order. March 24, 1999, the date of the first bombing attacks against the Belgrade regime, marked the beginning of the new era.

We knew that the Cold War had come to a close in November 1989 with the fall of the Berlin Wall, and that the disappearance of the Soviet Union in December 1991 had put an end to the post-war era. We now know that the Kosovo crisis put an end to a decade (1991–99) of uncertainty, disorder and trial and error in the domain of international politics, while also shaping a new framework for the 21st century.

Economic globalization — by far the most powerful dynamic of our times — needed a strategic global project as its complement in terms of security. The Kosovo conflict provided the occasion to produce the essential blueprint. From this standpoint, NATO's *first* war was in large part a "premiere." For the international community it represented a veritable leap into the unknown, an incursion into uncharted territory that would have many agreeable surprises in store but also more than one ambush and more than one danger.

With its pretext of the atrocities committed in Kosovo by the Belgrade regime, NATO justified its involvement in the conflict in humanitarian, moral and even "civilizing" terms: the French prime minister, Lionel Jospin, went so far as to declare that it was "a struggle for civilization."[18] History, culture and politics, the causes of all conflicts since the Punic Wars,[19] became obsolete references overnight. This was nothing less than a revolution, not only in military terms but also, and fundamentally, in intellectual terms. By engaging in the Kosovo War in the name of humanitarian action, which since then has been regarded as morally superior to all other justifications, NATO did not hesitate to violate two of the highest-order taboos of international politics: the sovereignty of states and the UN statutes.

THE PRINCIPLE OF SOVEREIGNTY

Under the *ancien régime*, sovereignty resided in the person of the monarch "by the grace of God." Thanks to the influence of the enlightenment philosophers, the 1776 American and 1789 French revolutions and all subsequent democracies, have had sovereignty reside with the people. "The principle of all sovereignty resides essentially in the nation," states Article 3 of the August 1789 Declaration of the Rights of Man and the Citizen.

This principle of sovereignty authorizes each government to resolve its internal conflicts in accordance with its own laws, which are drafted and promulgated by its own parliament, the seat of the nation's representatives. No one has the right to interfere with the internal affairs of the state in question. It was precisely this principle, now more than two centuries old, that went up in smoke on March 24, 1999, the date of the first bombing attacks on Serbia.

Some people say, and not mistakenly, that this is a good thing because, under the cover of a principle preventing other states coming to the aid of victims, more than one tyrannical state has committed all kinds of abuses against its own citizens. In the case of Yugoslavia many people consider that, even if Slobodan Milosevic was formally and democratically elected, he was still a despot who inspired a detestable policy of ethnic cleansing. Yet, the kind of legitimacy invoked by a despot, tyrant or dictator does not come from the people, and the sovereignty of his or her state is nothing but a legal artifice permitting arbitrary practises. Such sovereignty does not deserve the least respect, in particular if the despot in question is guilty of human rights violations or crimes against humanity.

We have recently seen how sovereign decisions, taken by the set of leading left-wing or right-wing political forces of a democratic country, can be blatantly disregarded. In Chile, the decisions made with regard to the former dictator General Augusto Pinochet, far from being respected, were not able to prevent his being detained in London. Neither did they deter Spain from requesting his extradition in order to try him for crimes against humanity.[20]

Similarly, the project of establishing the ICC (with the United States opposing its ratification) aims to try those who commit crimes against humanity, independently of any legal decision taken by a sovereign state.

TOWARD THE INDIVIDUAL-STATE?

Globalization, apart from breaking down borders, homogenizing cultures and reducing differences, does not fit well with the identity and sovereignty of states. As Alain Joxe notes, "The constitution of a universal empire (of the United States) through the generalization of the market economy is producing Balkanizations-liberalizations in eliminating the regulating prerogatives of traditional states."[21]

Where does the sovereignty of a country reside today? Are we heading for the installation of "limited sovereignties," on a planetary scale and under the aegis of the West, like those that Leonid Brezhnev and the Soviet Union tried to impose on the states of the socialist bloc in the 1970s? Should we judge in this light the resurrection of the old colonial form of the "protectorate," which was envisaged in 1991 for Somalia, practised de facto in Albania and again, under UN auspices, in Kosovo, Afghanistan and Iraq in the guise of a multinational force?[22]

At the end of the 18th century, sovereignty shifted from God to the nation. Will it now shift to reside in the individual? After the nation-state, are we now going to see the emergence of the "individual-state"? Will the attributes and prerogatives that have hitherto characterized states be passed on to specific individuals? There is no doubt that globalization and its ideology will not only tolerate but will encourage such a transformation, now made possible by information and communications technology, as Osama Bin Laden and his network-sect al-Qaida have demonstrated (see Chapter 1, which deals with the events of September 11).

SIDELINING THE UNITED NATIONS

NATO decided to go to war over Kosovo without the explicit authorization of any UN Security Council resolution. For the first time ever, and in such a serious matter, we saw the sidelining of the only international platform for the resolution of conflicts and maintenance of peace.

Since the early 1990s, there have been many signs that the United States wants the United Nations to stop performing its international role. Butros Butros Ghali's mandate was not renewed and he was replaced by Kofi Annan, presumably more malleable in Washington's terms. The Dayton Agreements on Bosnia were signed, not under the aegis of the United Nations but that of the United States, as happened with the Wye River Palestine-Israeli Agreements, and the decision to bomb Iraq was unilateral, without UN authorization.

In fact, everything suggests that the United States is not happy with the United Nations. In its present hegemonic position, it does not accept any obstacles that might be raised by the legalistic procedures of the United Nations. It is clear, then, that the existence of the United Nations throughout the 20th century (initially in the form of the League of Nations) was not due to an "achievement of civilization." Instead it was simply a confluence of powers with comparable spheres of influence, so that (at least in military terms) none of them could impose on the others.

The disappearance of the Soviet Union upset this balance. For the first time in centuries, one country — a "hyperpower" according to Hubert Védrine, the former French minister for foreign affairs — is overwhelmingly dominating the world. The United States sees no reason to share or limit its hegemony when it can be so clearly exercised without restrictions, with no one (not even the United Nations) able to object.

Committed in the name of humanitarianism, these two transgressions — one against national sovereignty and the other against UN authority — have raised several issues. For example, how can humanitarian concerns be reconciled with the use of force? Can "ethical bombing attacks" be carried out, especially when numerous errors result in hundreds of civilian victims? Is it possible to speak of a "just war" when the military and technological imbalance between the adversaries is so vast? In the name of what morality can the legitimate protection of the Kosovars be compared with the destruction of the Serbs?

WAR AND ECOLOGY

These questions are uncomfortable for present-day social democratic leaders, former children of 1968, Trotskyists, Maoists, communists, pacifists etc. They were part of the Love Generation and Flower Power, shouting "Make love not war," singing antimilitarist songs (see Donovan, *Universal Soldier*) and fiercely opposing the Vietnam War. According to these leaders' present stance, Vietnam would now be a "just cause."

Some European environmental leaders, in particular the German Greens, found it a tough job to reconcile their traditional discourse about protecting the environment with their warmongering positions. They eventually acknowledged that the Kosovo War, like any war, was in itself an ecological catastrophe. We need only consider the destruction of oil refineries with the consequent emission of clouds of toxic gases; the bombing of chemical factories that then contaminated rivers and wiped out fauna; the use of graphite bombs that released carcinogenic dust and of radioactive depleted uranium bombs; the dropping of scatter bombs with their thousands of devices that blow up like antipersonnel mines (the United States refused to sign the Ottawa Treaty that prohibited their use); and the activated bombs that were dropped into the Adriatic, where they now constitute a threat to fishermen.

Others wonder why NATO did not intervene, for humanitarian reasons, in other countries whose populations are also subjugated, for example the south of Sudan, Sierra Leone, Liberia, the Congo, Angola, West Papua, Tibet, etc. Others note that humanitarianism is not free of double standards; Iraq was bombed daily by the United States and Britain throughout all of 1999, without the backing of any international mandate. Finally, with respect to the right of humanitarian intervention, some critics have indicated that this should not only be the right of the strongest. Yet, how could the weak exercise such a right? Should we suppose, for example, that an African country could invoke this right of humanitarian intervention in the United States, aiming to protect the rights of African Americans who are victims of human rights violations? Or might a North African country intervene in a European state, where migrants from the Maghreb are the subjects of systematic discrimination?

Why not demand, as some people have, the right of social intervention? Is it not a scandal when there are 50 million poverty-stricken people in the European Union? Is this not a monstrous violation of human rights? Is it acceptable, on the worldwide scale, that one out of every two human beings has to live on less than one euro a day? At this rate, the €60 million NATO spent daily in their bombing of Yugoslavia could have been used to feed 60 million people, per day.

THE ECOSYSTEM IN DANGER
NEW THREATS, NEW FEARS

6

"In the history of human communities," states the French philosopher Jean Delumeau, "fears change, but fear persists."[1] Until the 20th century, the great disasters of humanity had their origins in nature: cold, rigors of the climate, floods, catastrophes, fire, hunger, and scourges like the plague, cholera, tuberculosis and syphilis. In the past, humans lived under the constant threat of the environment. Calamity stalked humans every day of their lives.

The first half of the 20th century was marked by the horrors of the two world wars, bringing death on an industrial scale, exodus, massive destruction, persecution, deportation and death camps. After World War II and the atomic destruction of Hiroshima and Nagasaki, the world lived under the threat of nuclear holocaust. This fear slowly waned as the Cold War ended and international treaties that prohibited nuclear proliferation were signed.

NUCLEAR TERROR

The existence of these treaties, however, did not eliminate all the dangers. On April 26, 1986, the explosion at the Chernobyl nuclear power station caused nuclear terrors to flare up again. More recently, on October 1, 1999, there was an accident at the nuclear power plant in the Japanese town of Tokaimura. International public opinion was forced to confront the awful truth: even in a country like Japan, renowned for its technical rigor, elementary security norms are not being observed, and the lives and health of hundreds of millions of people are at risk.

Immediately afterwards, on October 13, 1999, it was announced that the U.S. Senate had made the incredible decision not to ratify the Comprehensive Test Ban Treaty (CTBT), acting against the wishes of President Bill Clinton. This refusal, arising from niggardly political considerations, is extremely serious. It represents nothing less than disaster for the security of the whole planet, especially when it could be interpreted as a tacit, generalized authorization for nuclear testing. It is an attack on the principle of nuclear nonproliferation,[2] and casts strong doubt that Washington may exert any future pressure to stop nuclear testing.

At the end of 2001, and despite Moscow's demurral, it was Washington once again that repudiated the 1972 treaty on limiting the deployment of antiballistic missiles (ABM). This treaty had been drawn up as a precaution against progress being made in the ballistic field in particular countries (such as Pakistan, Iran and North Korea). Once the U.S. Senate had voted against it, Russia and China, neither of which had ratified the CTBT, now had a good pretext to continue with new tests, aiming to streamline their arsenals as France had done in 1995.

Former French prime minister, Lionel Jospin, "bearing in mind the ballistic weapons and the weapons of mass destruction that certain powers are acquiring," declared that he was prepared to consider "modernizing" and "modifying" the French nuclear arsenal. This would "prevent the appearance of any threat against our vital interests, whatever its origin (near or far), nature or form might be."[3] As were other countries, Jospin was doubtless thinking about Pakistan, a young nuclear power whose democratically elected civilian authorities had been ousted on October 12, 1999, by the army headed by General Pervez Musharraf.

In Western Europe, the latter half of the 20th century was characterized by a progressive reduction of armed conflicts and an almost generalized increase in prosperity. There was a notable improvement in standards of living, while life expectancy figures climbed to unprecedented heights.

On the day when historians of the mind ask themselves about human fears at the start of the 21st century, they will discover that, terrorism aside, our new fears are less political or military (conflicts, persecution, wars) than economic and social (stock exchange disasters, hyperinflation, bankruptcy of enterprises, massive dismissals, social instability, extensive poverty), industrial (accidents as serious as those in Minamata, Seveso, Bhopal and Toulouse) or ecological (disorders in nature, deterioration of the environment, food quality effecting health, pollution of all kinds). They affect both collective and personal spheres of life (health, food) and our human identity (artificial procreation, genetic engineering).

The latter aspect is increasingly alarming, because our capacity to manipulate humanity's genetic constitution is greater than ever. The production of transgenic animals, cloning, human genome sequencing, gene therapy, patenting of life forms, genetic identification of hereditary diseases and the use of genetic testing are giving rise to great concern.[4]

We should recall certain ideas voiced in the United States in the 1960s and 1970s: researchers like Dr. José Delgado, one of the strongest proponents of mind control in the interests of attaining a "psycho-civilized" society, asserted that the essential philosophical question was not, "What is man?" but, "What kind of man are we going to manufacture?"

Professor Marvin Minsky, one of the founders of the computer, has forecast that, "In 2035, thanks to nanotechnology, the electronic equivalent of the brain might be smaller than a fingertip. This means that you could have inside your brain all the space you want to implant additional systems and memories. Like this, little by little, you could learn more things every year, add new types of perceptions, new forms of reasoning, new ways of thinking and imagining."[5]

The U.S. essayist Francis Fukuyama asserts that, "in the course of the next two generations, biotechnology will provide the tools to achieve what the specialists in social engineering have so far failed to do. At that stage we shall have definitively gone beyond human history because, by then, we shall have abolished human beings as such. A new history will then begin, beyond what we know as human."[6]

SCIENCE AND FICTION

Ever since the cloning of Dolly the sheep in February 1997, it has become evident that the cloning of human beings is just around the corner. Science has superceded fiction, to the extent that it has gone well beyond "Bokanovsky's process" described by Aldous Huxley in *Brave New World*. Dolly was not the result of conception as it was previously understood. Her embryo was created simply by taking the nucleus of an adult cell and transferring it to an ovum of a surrogate mother sheep from which the nucleus had been removed. Since then, mice have been cloned in Hawaii, sheep in New Zealand and Japan and goats in the United States. By 1998, *The Lancet* was arguing that, despite mounting international concern, the creation of human beings by means of cloning had become "inevitable," and it called upon the medical community to admit it once and for all.

It was in this atmosphere that, on June 26, 2000, the media announced the start of a new era: scientists had succeeded in decoding some three billion DNA base pairs on the 23 chromosomes that are the sum of our inherited genetic constitution. This will now enable the sequencing of the genes involved in various human illnesses. This has huge potential benefits for humanity, as the identification of the gene responsible for any given hereditary illness would open the way to discovering a possible treatment and cure.

We are, however, a long way from understanding the full implications of this discovery and the unforeseen dangers it brings. Genetics is now making it possible for humanity to embark upon a "wholesale appropriation of the world, a modern version of the slavery and plundering of natural resources that characterized the colonial enterprise."[7] The fact is that patenting genes is tantamount to privatizing the common heritage of humanity. The selling of such information to the pharmaceutical industry — thereby restricting its availability to the privileged few — threatens to transform a revolutionary scientific breakthrough into yet another source of discrimination.[8]

As if this were not enough, genetic engineering is the harbinger of a new kind of eugenics, geared toward forms of "transhumanity." Should we not interpret this as a resurgence of the notion of creating "perfect children," selected in terms of the excellence of their genetic coding? Our societies hardly dare to acknowledge it. A lurking and unspoken fear is beginning to take shape: are we on the verge of producing the human species on a factory production-line? Are we going to end up making human or transhuman Pokémons?[9] Are we about to see an invasion of GMHs, genetically modified humans?

NEOLIBERALISM AND ECOLOGY

The genetic manipulation that is already underway is not the only factor disturbing to citizens. Ecological warnings, such as those expressed at the 1992 Earth Summit in Rio de Janeiro and at the World Summit on Sustainable Development, held in Johannesburg in July–August 2002, have also alerted them to the risks involved in the present-day ravaging of the planet.

Aiming to allay these fears and discuss the measures that should be taken in response to global warming, the result of increased emission of greenhouse-effect gases, representatives from 150 countries met in the Japanese city of Kyoto in 1997. The fact that this crucial conference was held when Asia was submerged in a series of financial and ecological disasters should not be overlooked. The old "dragons" (Hong Kong, Singapore, Taiwan and South Korea) and the new (Malaysia, Indonesia, Thailand and the Philippines) have long been presented as the counter example to the so-called failure of the Third World. The world's leading economic institutions — the World Bank, IMF, OECD and WTO — and the acolytes of ultra-liberalism had declared them to be a model to be imitated. Yet in the autumn of 1997, the "dragons" were undergoing a series of major stock market upheavals.

After the collapse of the Hong Kong Stock Exchange, the finance markets of the five continents, starting with Wall Street, were sucked into the whirlwind. Once again, the specter of an international monetary crash began to loom. This model of growth is based on cheap labor, heavily devalued currency, massive exports and increased interest rates to attract international investors-speculators, all within the framework of authoritarian political regimes. After the 1997 Asian debacle, all this was revealed as being not exemplary but dangerous.

To make matters worse, two of the countries most affected by the stock market typhoons — Indonesia and Malaysia — were faced with ecological disasters of staggering proportions. Uncontrolled fires devastated more than 800,000 hectares of tropical forest in the islands of Sumatra, Borneo, Java and Sulawesi. Huge clouds of toxic smoke, the size of half a continent, smothered cities as large as Kuala Lumpur with soot, leaving them in semidarkness. Serious accidents subsequently occurred (an Airbus crash with 234 dead, and a collision at sea with 29 dead).

MASSIVE DEFORESTATION

Needless to say, these two catastrophes — economic and environmental — are closely related. Although it is true that the fires were partly the result of drought caused by the cyclic climatic phenomenon El Niño, the main reason for the disaster lay in a policy of massive deforestation. Over decades, it has been an intrinsic part of the logic of a speculative, highly over-productive and suicidal model that was concerned only with export.

In the name of a self-serving confusion between "growth" and "development," the states of both North and South persist in their systematic destruction of the environment. Their attacks on the land, water and atmosphere are occurring with no thought to the future. Galloping urbanization, destruction of tropical forests, pollution of aquifers, seas and rivers, global warming, impoverishment of the ozone layer, acid rain: these ecological disasters endanger the future of humanity.

Each year six million hectares of arable land disappear thanks to desertification. All around the world, erosion and overexploitation are consuming the arable surface of the Earth at an accelerated pace. The industrial contamination of the developed countries and the poverty of the underdeveloped countries (deforestation, neglect of fallow land, etc.) are upsetting the ecological balance. Absurd economic and political policies are leading to the deaths of millions of human beings from hunger.

PROTECTING BIODIVERSITY

By 2010, the forest cover of the Earth will have diminished by more than 40 percent from 1990. By 2040, the accumulation of greenhouse-effect gases could cause a rise between one and two degrees centigrade in the Earth's average temperature, along with a rise in sea level of between 0.2 and 1.5 meters. This is not absolutely certain, but if we wait for scientific confirmation it will already be too late to act, and irreparable damage would already have been caused.

Every year, between 10 and 17 million hectares of forestland disappears. Deforestation is destroying an irreplaceable biological heritage: rainforests are home to 70 percent of the animal species, 6,000 of which are wiped off the face of the Earth every year. According to the World Conservation Union (IUCN), 20 percent of the world's existing species will have disappeared within 10 years.

The Berlin Climate Change Conference, held in April 1995, reinforced the idea that the market was not the right vehicle for confronting these global threats to the environment. Protecting biodiversity through sustainable development has become imperative, and development can only be considered sustainable if it permits future generations to inherit an environment of at least the same quality as that enjoyed by earlier generations.

The countries of the West must respect the commitments made at the Rio de Janeiro Earth Summit in 1992. The United States must pay particular attention, as this single nation is responsible for half of the emission of carbon gases from the industrialized countries. At present they do not. While the European Union envisaged a reduction of 15 percent in these gases by 2010, the U.S. Administration merely proposes to return to its 1990 levels by 2012 and to establish negotiable "contamination permits" after 2008. President George W. Bush has been even more recalcitrant. One of the first measures taken by his administration, to the great dismay of governments around the world, was to repudiate the Kyoto Protocol.

Many Third World governments refuse to accept that the degradation of their ecosystems has tragic consequences for humanity as a whole. Yet it is evident that we are not going to be able to take the burden from the Earth without collective effort. The bell has tolled in both the developed and underdeveloped worlds, warning that it is high time we abandoned the model of development we have pursued for centuries to the immense misfortune of the Earth and its inhabitants.

This attitude is characteristic of the selfishness that is the norm today. It is encouraged more than ever by globalization for, *inter alia*, globalization means the ecological plunder of the Earth on a worldwide scale. It is a despoliation that sets off chain reactions. From Mozambique to Venezuela, from China to Turkey, from Mexico to India, calamities, cataclysms, floods and earthquakes have been occurring in recent years to an extent never seen before.

Thousands of dead, billions of euros spent on repairing damage and unimaginable ecological disasters: devastated forests, decimated fauna, lost crops, polluted waters, ruined arable land. In the dev-

eloped countries — generally better protected from "natural" calamities — climatic disturbances have had dramatic effects. We need go
no further than Eastern Europe, lashed by two hurricanes in December 1999 that left hundreds dead, colossal, unprecedented damage
and highly traumatized populations in the regions affected.

Developed countries, which believed they were immune to the
calamities affecting the countries of the South, have also suffered the
consequences of new ecological disturbances. We need only recall
what has happened in Europe over the last several years.

We began with the horrific oil slick that spread along the Atlantic
coast of France in December 1999. Caused by the wreck of the tanker
Erika that had been chartered by the oil company Total, it killed
thousands of birds, endangered hundreds of businesses and ruined
one of the country's most beautiful regions. The volunteers who
participated in cleaning up the beaches were exposed to the risk of
carcinogenic contamination.

Other catastrophes were the repeated flooding of the River Somme
in the north of France, and countless problems arising from food
contamination: the discovery that human excrement was being used
in the manufacture of fodder for animals and fish raised for human
consumption; new cases of mad cow disease; dioxin-contaminated
chickens; contaminated Coca-Cola cans and bottles of mineral water;
a proliferation of genetically manipulated products; food poisoning
among people who had consumed cheeses or sausages with listeria
contamination, etc.

In the name of an erroneous conception of development, most
states in the developed world continue to comply with the frenetic
demands of production-oriented policies. In practical terms, this
means an abusive resort to pesticides and other pollutants, to the
detriment of traditional and biological agriculture. Meanwhile, many
countries in the underdeveloped world, whether they are unaware
or simply impotent, continue to tolerate the systematic destruction
of their environments.

Across the globe, all kinds of outrages and attacks are being committed against the earth, its water systems, the atmosphere and the health of human beings: uncontrolled urbanization, the logging of tropical forests, contamination of seas and rivers, global warming, holes in the ozone layer, acid rain and so on. Ecological disasters, because of their mammoth scope, now constitute a danger to the future of humanity itself.

A NEW PLAGUE

"Plague," writes Antonin Artaud, "is a manifestation of the depths of latent cruelty that bring together, in an individual or a people, all the perverse possibilities of the spirit."[10] Like the plague, the epizootic foot-and-mouth disease that swept the British countryside in spring 2001 also revealed those "depths of latent cruelty" and many "perverse possibilities of the spirit." Epidemics, as all historians confirm, do not derive from a single cause but are the result of a specific historical conjuncture.

It is not by chance, then, that an England that had served as a laboratory for ultraliberalism for more than 20 years, should have witnessed the macabre spectacle of widespread medieval-style bonfires. Hundreds of thousands of animals — uselessly, as it turned out[11] — were sacrificed to the flames amid cries of horror and despair. To the great misfortune of British citizens, this nightmare was the last straw of the winter of 2000–01, which had been prodigious in its calamities: mad cow disease, floods, regions cut off by snow and without power, railway disasters, etc. There is no divine curse, no "conspiracy of destiny"[12] to explain such a spate of disasters.

The decisions that led to these dramas were very consciously taken, obeying specific dogmas straight from the neoliberal catechism. The wildfire spread of foot-and-mouth disease was due to the pursuit of profits, pushing operators to cut costs (and therefore safety measures). In the 1980s, the successive Thatcher governments rejected the principle of prevention and dismantled the national veterinarian network, in the name of deregulation. As if that were not enough, another decision was made, one that was to have terrible consequences: in order to save millions of pounds and to favor exports, vaccination of animals was now prohibited.

These two measures, true to the logic of production-oriented agriculture, created the conditions for the epizootic outbreak. As it was now forbidden to apply the advances made in veterinary medicine after Pasteur, the struggle against the spread of the outbreak had to resort to archaic methods. They could only be inspired by the Hippocratic maxim *"Cito, longe, tarde"* (at once, for a long way, and for a long time), applied in antiquity against all epidemics. Adopted as a kind of "agriculture without borders," these measures ushered in a rigorous protectionism. Yet it was also paradoxical, because one main factor had been overlooked: viruses ignore borders. In the age of globalization, they move from one place to another with an ease that is only comparable to capital flows, as one writer put it.[13]

GUILTY: COMPETITION

The obsession with competition and the breakneck race to obtain heftier and cheaper specimens are both at the origin of the outbreak of mad cow disease:

> All investigations reveal that there is a link between certain changes in the manufacturing process of rendered animal fodder in England and the appearance of the infectious prion protein. In 1981, British manufacturers skipped a phase in the manufacturing process: they lowered the temperature (to economize on energy) and left out solvents (to economize on raw materials). These two modifications made it more difficult to eradicate the disease and, indeed, helped to spread it.[14]

The same mindset induced the British Government to step up privatization after 1979. The sale of the railways to the private sector occurred in 1994. Since then, a series of accidents have caused 56 deaths and 730 injuries. The mass media accuse the new operators of sacrificing security to increase their profits and pander to their shareholders.

Did anything change in 1997 when Tony Blair and the Labor Party came to power? Nothing fundamental. His "third way" social democracy has turned out to be nothing more than a variant of what went before. Under his mandate, the GNP allocation for public spending is the lowest in 40 years. England has the crudest social contrasts in all of Europe. A low-profile privatization of the public education system continues. With increased university enrollment, Blair has introduced a selection system based on fees.

As for the health system, a WHO study placed the United Kingdom lowest in the European Union. Inequalities between rich and poor have increased. More than five million U.K. citizens live in conditions of the most abject poverty. Almost half of unwaged women work part-time. The standard of living of a quarter of the child population is below the poverty line. The United Kingdom has the highest number of poor children of all the industrialized countries.[15]

BROKEN PROMISES

These new fears — especially those relating to mad cow disease and GMO — also arise from disenchantment with technical advances. The utility of scientific progress is no longer as obvious as it once appeared, to the extent that its findings have been absorbed by the economic domain to become the instruments of companies greedy for profit.

The confusion between public and industrial interests has favored the latter on too many occasions. In the last 20 years, the rise of neoliberalism, worship of the market, the reappearance of highly unstable situations and new gulfs of social inequalities have only intensified the feeling that technical progress has not fulfilled its promise of improving the lot of all.

Nobody is unaware that the institutions (parliaments, governments and experts) that are supposed to guarantee security have failed time and again to deliver, especially during the mad cow disease crisis when their negligence and lack of foresight were evident for all to see. Moreover, public powers customarily put the collective interest on the line without any attempt to consult those concerned — in other words, the citizens — in open contempt of the democratic pact.[16]

What are the consequences? A tenacious suspicion has now taken hold of people's awareness; there is a growing reluctance to delegate the power to toy with the collective destiny to those "responsible," as their history of authorizing practises based on insufficiently tested and risky scientific innovations progressively undermines their citizens' faith. The sorcerers' apprentices of neo-science now have to confront growing mistrust.

Spectacular revelations about a number of "silent plagues" have demonstrated *a posteriori* the tragic incompetence of authorities and experts. We refer not only to cases of contaminated blood, but also to the asbestos scandal, which causes the deaths of some 10,000 workers every year in France. Then there are the infections picked up during hospital stays, which account for another 10 million deaths per year.[17] Air pollution, 60 percent of which is produced by traffic, is responsible for the trifling figure of 17,000 premature deaths per year.[18] Dioxin, a carcinogenic product released by domestic garbage incinerators, causes between 1,800 and 5,200 deaths per year.[19] One need only read the report on the epizootic outbreak of mad cow disease, released in the United Kingdom on October 26, 2000, to understand why European societies no longer have any faith in cattle products. Flying in the face of nature and scorning the most basic precautionary principles,[20] aberrant measures were adopted with the backing of "experts." When it became clear that the disease was spreading and being transmitted to human beings, the lies and subterfuges began. Predictably, the delays, evasions and denials, combined with the irresponsible attitude of the authorities, fed the suspicion that the British people had been deliberately misled. Given that the behavior of governments in the rest of Europe was no different, why should the citizens of the European Union not feel the same mistrust? This is particularly the case when they learn that, in France (to go no further), the commercialization of varieties of transgenic corn has been authorized despite the risks posed by GMOs?

Citizens are quite rightly disturbed by the priority given to economic groups and corporate egos, given the detrimental effect on the public interest. It is not that they are expecting to be offered total security and zero risk, but a clear definition of what might be an "acceptable risk" should concern everyone and not just the "experts."

THE GULF OF INEQUALITIES

We knew that the gulf of inequalities had stretched still deeper and wider in the course of the two ultraliberal decades (1979–2001), but how could we imagine the true extent of it? The three richest people in the world have accumulated between them a fortune that exceeds the GNPs of the 48 poorest countries, which is to say a quarter of all the states in the world. In more than 60 countries, the average income per inhabitant is less than it was 20 years ago. On the world scale, almost three billion people — half of humankind — live on less than €2 per day.

The abundance of goods has never been so great, yet the numbers of people without a roof over their heads, without work and without enough to eat are growing with no end in sight. About one third of the 4.5 billion inhabitants of the developing countries do not have access to drinking water. One fifth of the world's children do not consume enough calories and proteins. Some two billion people — a third of humanity — suffer from anemia.

Is this just the hand of destiny? Hardly. According to the United Nations, four percent of the wealth accumulated in the 225 greatest fortunes on earth would be sufficient to cover the basic needs (food, drinking water, education and health) of everyone in the world. The cost of meeting all the sanitary and nutritional needs of humankind would be €13 billion, slightly more than what the citizens of the United States and Europe spend on perfume.

The Universal Declaration of Human Rights, the 50th anniversary of which was celebrated in 1998, states that, "Everyone has the right to a standard of living adequate for the health and well-being of [themselves] and of [their] family, including food, clothing, housing and medical care and necessary social services."[21] Yet, these rights are evermore inaccessible for the greater part of humanity.

THE GEOPOLITICS OF HUNGER

Let us take, for example, the right to food. It is not true that there is a lack of food. It has never been so abundant. There is enough for each of the planet's six billion inhabitants to access at least 2,700 calories a day. However, simply producing food is not enough. All human groups must have the wherewithal to buy and consume it. Naturally, this is not the case. Every year, 30 million people die of hunger; 800 million suffer from chronic malnutrition.

There is nothing irremediable about this either. The ravages of climatic disturbances tend to be predictable. When they are able to intervene, organizations like Action Against Hunger (*Action contre le faim*)[22] can step in to prevent an incipient shortage of food in a matter of weeks. Nonetheless, hunger continues to decimate whole populations.

Why is this so? Hunger has become a political weapon. In fact there is no such thing as a chance famine. Unscrupulous leaders and organizations, finding themselves deprived of a source of income when the Cold War came to an end, now practise nothing less than a strategy of hunger. As Sylvie Brunel puts it:

> Those who have been condemned to hunger are not enemy peoples any more, nor are they nations to be conquered. They belong to the very same populations as certain other people who wish to turn this bonanza of conflicts to their own benefit. These conflicts represent access to media projection and its corollary, opening the floodgates of international compassion to obtain an inexhaustible supply of funds, food and international platforms from which they can voice their claims.[23]

In Somalia, Sudan, Liberia, North Korea, Burma and Afghanistan, government officials and warlords hold their own populations to ransom and let them die of hunger for their own political ends. At times this occurs with the most appalling cruelty. In Sierra Leone where soldiers of the Rebel United Front, led by a former corporal of the Sierra Leone Army, Foday Sankoh, engaged in a horrific terror campaign for years, systematically amputating the hands of peasants so that they could not cultivate their crops. At present, the role of the climate in causing famine is marginal: the culprits are human beings, who make other human beings die of hunger.

Well known for his writings demonstrating that some politicians are capable of causing hunger among their populations even when food is abundant, Professor Amartya Sen, the 1998 Nobel Prize laureate for Economics, has stated, "One of the most notable facts of the terrible history of hunger is that there has never been a serious lack of food in any country with a democratic form of government and a relatively free press."[24]

Contrary to neoliberal thinking, Professor Sen holds that the leading role in ensuring the well-being of a society should correspond to the state and not to the market. The state should be sensitive to the needs of all its citizens, while being responsible, on a planetary scale, for the development of humanity as a whole.

TERROR OF DISEASE

One hundred years ago, scientists and doctors were very optimistic about the radiant future of public health as it was heralded by advances in hygiene and the Pasteur revolution. There is no doubt that the world has advanced in terms of collective health, but this progress is overshadowed by the existence of the most outrageous of scandals: tremendous inequalities in access to medical attention. Gro Harlem Brundtland, director general of the WHO, has noted that, "More than one billion people will enter the 21st century without ever having benefited from the health revolution: their lives are brief and marked by illness."[25]

With regard to access to available medicines, and research into treatment of diseases that are either nonexistent or of little importance in the developed countries, the gulf separating the poor countries from the rich grows ever deeper. Among the main threats that will affect human health in the 21st century is cardiovascular disease, which is mainly related to metabolic disturbances — hypercholesterol, obesity, diabetes, etc. It is increasingly common due to the spread of the western lifestyle, in other words, a diet abundant in fats and not enough physical exercise.

Infectious diseases, however, will have a growing incidence and will take tens of millions of lives every year. This will especially be the case in poor countries, but since we now live in a global village, we can expect a boomerang effect so that the diseases endemic to the poor countries will also affect the developed countries. One third of the world's deaths in 2001 were caused by serious infectious diseases like tuberculosis, AIDS, cholera, gastroenteritis in children, malaria, etc.

The rapid growth of the world's population and the birth of megacities, surrounded by universes of immigrants, the underprivileged and socially excluded people, have produced a breeding ground of emergency situations and the reemergence of some diseases. Globalization is accelerating the propagation of infectious diseases.

Nowadays, diseases travel and so do resistant bacteria. Once, the health risk was confined to the locus of the outbreak, but today diseases spread extraordinarily quickly. Thanks to globalization, bacteria travel at the speed of aircraft. Germs that have adapted to the conditions of life among a resistant population can spread among populations that are not prepared and thus highly vulnerable. Viruses circulate at the speed of charter flights and tourist groups, transmitting cholera, yellow fever, dengue fever, influenza and, lamentably, HIV/AIDS.

THE GEOGRAPHY OF AIDS

AIDS is now among the world's 10 leading causes of mortality. In view of increase in cases of HIV infection, it could soon come to be among the top five causes of death worldwide. At present it is estimated that there are some 36 million HIV-positive people in the world and more than 24 million of these live in Africa. Most of them will die within the next 10 years. To these must be added the other 14 million Africans who have already died of AIDS. At the end of 2001, about 18 million people (adults and children) had died of AIDS since the disease first appeared. In 2001 alone, 2.5 million people died.

About 95 percent of the new AIDS cases appear in the Third World, among people who have no means to stop the development of the disease. This presages an increase in the number of AIDS deaths in the coming years. It is calculated that, in 2001 alone, there were 5.6 million new cases; 570,000 of these were children under 15; 90 percent of them were African. This is equivalent to 15,000 new cases per day.

In western and southern Africa, 90 percent of those infected are unaware of the fact. About 11.5 million children around the world are orphans because of AIDS; 80 percent of them live in Africa; 55 percent of the adults infected in sub-Saharan Africa are women, and the chances that an African girl between 15 and 19 years is HIV positive are five to six times higher than for a boy in the same age group.

The greatest increase for HIV infection worldwide now appears in the newly independent states of the former Soviet Union. Between 1997 and 2000, the HIV-positive population doubled. In Eastern Europe, the number of cases has risen by a third, to reach some 360,000 people. In Asia, at the end of 2001, about seven million people (or five times more than the figures for AIDS deaths at that point) were carriers of the virus. In China, despite cover-ups by authorities, it is estimated that there are several million infected people. Given the increase in numbers of intravenous drugs users sharing syringes, an explosion in the number of people infected is to be feared. In contrast, the prevention programs in India, Thailand and the Philippines have brought about a reduction or, at least, a fragile stabilization of the figures for HIV-positive people.

The scourge of AIDS has been advancing day by day for the last 20 years, slowly destroying the hopes of those who were sure that the spread of the disease could be stopped in its tracks once the killer HIV virus was identified. In 1993, World Bank experts calculated that the number of infected people around the world would rise to 26 million by 2000. At that point, they estimated that the virus would be killing about 1.8 million people per year. This forecast was described as pessimistic. However, WHO reports reveal, unfortunately, that the World Bank pundits underestimated the gravity of the situation, and that the AIDS epidemic has spread more rapidly and caused more deaths than they predicted.

All AIDS researchers confirm that the immense majority of those affected — about 95 percent — is concentrated in the poor countries of the South. There is no doubt that this proportion will rise in other countries where poverty, serious health system shortcomings and lack of resources for prevention and medical attention favor the propagation of the virus.

Sub-Saharan Africa and the developing countries of Asia, which together represent less than 10 percent of the world's GNP, are home to 89 percent of the total of HIV-positive people. Seventy percent of the total number of cases is concentrated in African countries alone, in other words 24 million HIV-positive people. Life expectancy in sub-Saharan Africa has dropped by seven years because of AIDS. In the nine most affected countries (where more than 10 percent of the adult population is HIV positive), life expectancy has dropped by 10 years. AIDS has now taken more lives than all the conflicts and all the wars of the last 10 years put together.

Most of those who are infected in the countries of the South will be dead in 10 years. They will leave devastated families behind them. Beyond the individual and family tragedies, however, there is no doubt that the epidemic will cause tremendous socioeconomic instability, not to mention political chaos. The prospects of development in a number of countries today are zero. In some countries of southern

Africa (Uganda, Zimbabwe, Zambia, Botswana and Malawi) one in every five people between 15 and 45 is HIV positive. In the continent as a whole, the population adversely affected by the epidemic — counting children and parents looking after AIDS sufferers — numbers more than 180 million.

As it spreads, AIDS will eat up more and more public and private resources, destabilizing production and economies, exhausting savings, exacerbating poverty and spawning wretchedness. It is calculated that in Kenya, for example, economic production will have dropped by 14.5 percent by 2005 because of the effects of the epidemic. By the same year, Ethiopia will have allocated 33 percent of its budget to treatment and care of AIDS patients; in Kenya it will be almost 50 percent and in Zimbabwe over 60 percent!

THE PLAGUE OF THE POOR

In these circumstances, international solidarity is contemptible for being so totally insufficient. In practise, no decisive steps have been taken to organize a common front against AIDS. This would be a struggle in which the money and the advances in diagnosis and treatment of the developed countries could come to the aid of the most underprivileged patients of the planet. Yet the dream of globalizing the fight against AIDS offers not even a glimpse of hope of becoming reality. Who in the developed countries would make the move to put an end to a plague that essentially affects the poor inhabitants of the poorest countries?

The amount allocated worldwide for the struggle against AIDS between 1990 and 1997 only increased from €165 million to €273 million. In the same period, the number of new cases more than trebled, going from 9.8 million people to 30.3 million people. According to the Joint UN Program on HIV/AIDS (UNAIDS), the amounts allocated per AIDS case between 1988 and 1997 by development aid organizations in the rich countries of the North, dropped by more than 50 percent in absolute value. The cost of preventing the spread of AIDS in the countries of the South varies between €1.20 and €3.50

per person per year, while the basic HIV treatment costs more than €7 per person per year. Naturally, the cost of effective treatment for the AIDS patient is astronomically higher.

According to the World Bank, the total sum needed for AIDS prevention in Africa fluctuates between €1 billion and €2.3 billion. Yet Africa only receives €160 million in official aid for the fight against AIDS. International action against this illness represents less than one percent of the annual official budgets for development aid of the rich countries. AIDS spectacularly symbolizes the abyss that exists between the rich and poor countries when it comes to access to treatment. For the latter, it is a three-fold problem: the prohibitive cost of some treatments; fluctuations in the provision of medicines; and insufficient research into diseases that only affect the poorest countries.

The cost of treatments makes them inaccessible to the immense majority of affected people. In Thailand, the cost of the triple therapy is €675, when a worker in the tertiary sector earns an average of €120 per month. In Kenya, the cost of the first two weeks of treatment for AIDS-associated meningitis is €800, but the average salary is less than €130 per month.

In the era of neoliberal globalization, not all individuals are equal with respect to AIDS, just as they are not in other domains. Rich and poor have different access to health services. Most of the latter continue to die while the former can be saved. Although the prospects of discovering a preventive vaccine are less and less rosy, the situation has changed since 1996. In some developed countries, the use of new protease inhibitor molecules, in association with inverse transcriptase inhibitors, has lowered mortality by 60 percent in four years.

In fact, the discovery of the triple therapy and the efficacy of new combinations of antiretroviral treatments, in addition to preventive measures, have halted the spread of the disease in developed countries. In Western Europe, for example, the number of new AIDS cases per year increased constantly until 1994, when the figure reached a ceiling of 25,000. Since then, thanks to the effectiveness of new treatments, it has progressively decreased so that by 1997 it was less than 15,000. The number of AIDS deaths dropped by 80 percent in four years thanks to the introduction of AIDS-polytherapy.

In the United States, the arrest of the disease has been no less spectacular: the statistics situate the reduction in the numbers of AIDS deaths, between the first quarter of 1996 and that of 1997, at 40 percent. All the epidemiological indicators show that, in the industrialized countries, AIDS is now on the way to becoming a chronic viral disease that is rarely fatal.

WAR AND AIDS

While HIV/AIDS is starting to recede in the rich countries, the epidemic tide continues to engulf the countries of the underdeveloped world. The figures for infection and death are still rising fast in most of the countries of Eastern Europe, Asia and central and southern Africa as well as in some Latin American countries (Peru, Venezuela, Colombia, Argentina and Chile).

Neither the rich countries nor the pharmaceutical companies are doing anything to redress this imbalance. "The pharmaceutical industry is in debt to AIDS sufferers and this debt should be paid," declares the head of one organization that works to combat HIV/AIDS. "For 15 years, the laboratories have made huge profits on our lives: today, when the epidemic has been tamed in the rich countries and is exploding in the poor ones, they are refusing to modify their strategies. They resist distributing the new medicines that are the last hope for those patients for whom all other treatments have failed."[26]

Kofi Annan, the UN secretary general, has exhorted the Security Council, precisely because it is the organ that is responsible for keeping the peace, to make the international struggle against HIV/AIDS an immediate priority. Peter Piot, head of UNAIDS, has said that conflicts and HIV are as united as a pair of diabolical twins. According to James Wolfensohn, president of the World Bank, with HIV/AIDS we are facing a war that is even more debilitating than war itself. Yet while every war requires a war fund, the international community is contributing nothing at all for this one.

All these declarations serve as a warning about the consequences of today's laissez-faire attitude. Where AIDS prevails, it destabilizes economies, engenders poverty and favors war. War, in turn, with all its crimes, rape, and chaos, facilitates the spread of the epidemic.

THE EMPIRE AGAINST IRAQ

Resolution 1441 on the disarmament of Iraq was unanimously adopted by the 15 members of the UN Security Council, which met in a public session in the New York headquarters on Friday, November 8, 2002. In Paragraph 13 it stated that Iraq "will face serious consequences as a result of its continued violations of its obligations."[1] In diplomatic terms, "serious consequences" meant military intervention. That is, Resolution 1441 implicitly authorized the war against Baghdad.

According to some, the fact that Saddam Hussein would have unconditionally accepted the return of UN weapons inspectors did not make the threat of conflict any less likely. Resolution 1441 did not give the Iraqi president any other option, as Paragraph 9 "demands that Iraq confirm within seven days of notification its intention to comply fully with this resolution; and demands further that Iraq cooperate immediately, unconditionally, and actively"[2] with the inspectors.

During the weeks before this resolution was voted on, a furious diplomatic debate set the United States and its principal allies (the United Kingdom, Italy and Spain) against France, Russia, Germany and the majority of Arab and Muslim countries. The controversy can be summarized as follows: Washington wanted one single resolution from the United Nations (effectively, Resolution 1441), authorizing the use of force were it demonstrated that Iraq held WMD. Paris and Moscow demanded that the Security Council should hold another meeting to draw up and vote on a new resolution, explicitly authorizing the use of force against Baghdad.

The Bush Administration got its way. Resolution 1441 alone permitted military intervention, on the grounds that the UN weapons inspectors discovered WMD. France and Russia finally gave in to the formidable pressure of the United States, having to content themselves with a consolatory phrase in Paragraph 12 which stated that the Security Council "decides to convene immediately upon receipt of a report [from the weapons inspectors] in order to consider the situation."[3] But this new meeting, a mere formality, could not have halted the effects of Resolution 1441, nor could it have cancelled the green light given to the military option on November 8, 2002.

In this way, the United Nations folded once more to the demands of Washington, and demonstrated that little can now be expected of it in terms of the impartiality of international law. The United Nations appears to be an arbitrator under the influence of its most powerful and demanding member state. In many parts of the world, respect for the United Nations has hit rock bottom. It is accused of measuring the world's problems according to whether one is an ally or an adversary of the United States.

The Bush Administration posed three main accusations against Saddam Hussein's regime: 1) it doesn't respect the resolutions of the United Nations; 2) it holds WMD; 3) it constitutes a threat to its neighbors. On these grounds, Resolution 1441 was voted in and the Hussein regime was threatened with imminent war. But the same treatment was not given to two of Washington's great allies, Pakistan and Israel: these states, we notice, do not respect even greater numbers of UN resolutions; hold nuclear, chemical and biological WMD;

and constitute a real threat to their neighbors (India and Palestine, respectively).

FEAR OF INTERNATIONAL TERRORISM

The U.S. Administration wants to avoid, by any means possible, an alliance being formed between an "outlaw regime" and "international terrorism." As early as 1997, under the Clinton Administration (1992–2000), the Secretary of Defense William Cohen expressed that fear:

> We face the possibility that regional actors... terrorist groups and even some religious sects will try to gain disproportionate power through the acquisition and use of weapons of mass destruction.

In January 1999, a public declaration by the leader of the al-Qaida network confirmed that the risk was very real. "Acquiring weapons for the defense of Muslims is a religious duty," said Osama Bin Laden. "If I have indeed acquired these weapons, then I thank God for enabling me to do so."[4] President Bush, in his speech to the United Nations on September 12, 2002, admitted that this possibility gave him sleepless nights: "Our greatest fear is that terrorists will find a shortcut to their mad ambitions when an outlaw regime supplies them with the technologies to kill on a massive scale."[5] In the mind of the U.S. president, this outlaw regime was Saddam Hussein's Iraq. And for that reason, with the aim of ending "international terrorism," he decided to attack Baghdad.

Although he won the war, it is far from certain that Bush ended what he calls terrorism. In the first place, the term "terrorism" is imprecise. For 200 years, it has been used indiscriminately to describe all those who resort, rightly or wrongly, to violent means to change the political order. Whether we like it or not, history shows that in certain cases, violence has been necessary.

A MORE PACIFIED WORLD

The media has often spoken of terrorism since September 11, 2001, but the reality of political violence has paradoxically diminished compared with the situation of a few years ago. In Latin America, for example, there was political violence and armed struggle until recently in El Salvador, Guatemala, Nicaragua and Peru; a little earlier, this violence was present in Uruguay, Argentina, Bolivia, Chile and Brazil. There was also political violence in the United States (the Black Panthers and Puerto Ricans) and in Canada (the Liberation Front of Quebec). All of this has disappeared, and the only case which continues is that of Colombia, which began in 1948.

The same has occurred in Africa, where the political violence has largely disappeared from Mozambique, South Africa, Angola, Sierra Leone, Chad, Ethiopia and Eritrea. It still continues in Algeria, the south of Sudan, the Congo, Liberia and the Ivory Coast. In Asia, we have seen the end of the terrible wars in Vietnam, Cambodia, Laos and the guerrilla fighting in East Timor. Still in evidence, though, are the conflicts of Kashmir, Sri Lanka and the Philippines and the recent outbreak of Maoist guerrilla violence in Nepal.

In the Middle East, the cruel war in Lebanon has ended, and the Islamic Shi'ite organization Hizbullah has practically ceased its military actions after the withdrawal of Israel from Southern Lebanon. Only the Israel-Palestine conflict continues with its tragic balance of cruelties and civilian victims from both sides.

In Europe, excluding the Caucasus region where the Chechnyan conflict continues, the wars in Bosnia, Croatia, Kosovo and Macedonia have ended, as has the political violence in Turkish Kurdistan. The Red Brigades in Italy, the Red Army Faction (Baader-Meinhof Gang) in Germany, and even the IRA in Northern Ireland have currently laid down their arms. All that remains, unfortunately, is ETA in the Spanish Basque region.

Compared with previous decades, today's world appears to be infinitely more pacified. With the exception of five or six focus points (including the hazy sect-network of al-Qaida), political violence and terrorism have diminished on the geopolitical map. Yet we do not have that impression. First, because in many places this violence continues to kill; and second, because at the international level the United States has declared an "infinite war" against terrorism, and the media sound box, emanating from the all-powerful U.S. media, repeats the cry ad nauseum.

In reality, we ought to be happy that there is so little political violence in the world today. Instead, the world created by neoliberal globalization over the last 15 years, with the complicity of so many leaders, is one of unprecedented social violence and inequality. More than half of the world's inhabitants live on less than €2 a day. Thirty thousand people (10 times the number of victims of the attacks of September 11) die *every day* after drinking poor quality water. Thirty million people die of hunger every year, when world agricultural production is so abundant that it could feed up to eight billion people. For lack of medication, one boy or girl dies of an easily curable illness *every three seconds.*

Compared with the tremendous misery and the infinite injustice which the majority of the world's population suffers, isn't it actually paradoxical that there is so little political violence? There is no proof of complicity between the authors of the hateful attacks of September 11, 2001, and the regime of Saddam Hussein. Neither the U.S. nor the British authorities, have been able to establish — not even after military victory — a nexus between the al-Qaida network and Saddam Hussein. They therefore cannot present the attack on Iraq as a part of "the war on international terrorism."

SPREADING DEMOCRACY?

Doubtless influenced by the dominant propaganda, certain "experts" claim that Washington will effectively intervene not only in Iraq, but throughout the entire region, aiming to clear out each and every dictatorship. The liquidation of Saddam Hussein would only be the first example. They invite us to applaud such an undertaking as the "democratization of the Arab world." In a way, they tell us, the ends (coming democracy) justify the means (preemptive war).

This fairytale cannot be believed by anyone who has a minimal understanding of the history of U.S. military interventions in countries formerly known as the Third World. The United States has sown dictatorships all over the world. This has principally been in Central America and the Caribbean, where few have forgotten the bloody tyrannies of Batista in Cuba, Trujillo in Santo Domingo, Duvalier in Haiti, Somoza in Nicaragua, Ríos Montt in Guatemala, Pérez Jiménez in Venezuela, Stroessner in Paraguay, Videla in Argentina and Pinochet in Chile, to cite some of the most tragic examples.

In the Middle East, the project to establish a democracy in Iraq is scarcely credible, given that Washington has supported, in some cases for decades, some of the most frightening autocracies in the region: Egypt (one of the countries with the world's most political prisoners, more than 20,000), Saudi Arabia (a principal center of Islamic radicalism), the Arab Emirates, Pakistan (which protected the Taliban for years) and Uzbekistan.

The maxim fed to us by the propaganda is excellent: to die for democracy. The reality is much more prosaic: to conquer Iraqi oil. The true objective of the assault on Baghdad was oil. All other objectives were mere pretexts. The United Nations knew it. It also knew that the United States would have attacked with or without Resolution 1441. On November 10, 2002, two days after the Security Council's historic vote, Andrew Card, general secretary of the White House, declared to the press, "The United Nations can meet and discuss, but we don't need their permission."

BUSH'S HAWKS

The hawks who surround President Bush have long desired this war against Iraq. Who are these hawks? There are four main ones: Vice-President Dick Cheney; Secretary of Defense Donald Rumsfeld; Pentagon's number two Paul Wolfowitz; and the president of the Defense Policy Board, Richard Perle, nicknamed "The Prince of Darkness." These men — together with Condoleezza Rice, Bush's adviser on security questions, and, to a certain degree, Secretary of State Colin Powell — constitute the true council of war.

These are four dangerous men, and none of them, paradoxically, has ever fought in any wars. All of them arranged to avoid going to Vietnam. At the end of the 1980s they had gathered around President Bush Snr. Fifteen years after the end of the Vietnam War which so traumatized U.S. citizens, they were the first to theorize the use of war as an instrument of foreign policy.

The first great political adventure of this infernal quartet was the invasion of Panama in December 1989, without the authorization of the United Nations or even the U.S. Congress. Cheney, Rumsfeld, Wolfowitz and Perle (with Colin Powell as chairman of the Joint Chiefs of Staff) devised, from beginning to end, operation "Just Cause": a military invasion of Panama, overthrowing the "autocrat" Manuel Noriega and "establishing democracy" by giving power to their protégé Guillermo Endara. They wrote the script which consisted of launching a media campaign to demonize Noriega (formerly on the CIA payroll), qualifying him as a "drug trafficker," "pornographer," a "practitioner of voodoo witchcraft," and, obviously, a "dictator addicted to torture and a violator of human rights."

Once public opinion was prepared, the attack occurred: sudden, massive and without witnesses. The press was not advised of the offensive, in fact, some U.S. commandos shot down a Spanish photographer from the newspaper *El País* for his curiosity. The United States deployed the storm troopers from the military bases of the Canal Zone, which was then in the possession of the United States. They used, for the first time, the F117-A Stealth Bombers. While targeting Noriega's headquarters in Panama City they "erroneously" bombed the populated district of Chorrillo, causing close to 2,000 deaths. These deaths inaugurated what has since become known as "collateral damage." The United Nations condemned this aggression, but the U.S. ambassador used his veto power in the Security Council.

With the victory in Panama, Bush Snr.'s team of hawks had demonstrated that war was not a high risk option, but merely an acceptable method of diplomatic regulation. These four "tough men" achieved what they set out to do: they returned the U.S. Armed Forces to the status of a fundamental tool in U.S. foreign policy. From here on, the military might of the United States would be at the service of a project of global imperial domination.

It was these men who planned the Gulf War in 1991, and these men who were left frustrated as President Bush Snr. did not allow his troops to continue their offensive into Baghdad itself.

During the Clinton years, these hawks took refuge in universities or study centers where they continued to defend their thesis. The toughest of the four, Paul Wolfowitz, nicknamed "the Velociraptor," expounded their main political conclusions of the Gulf War in a memorandum published in 1992. Eleven years ago and long before the attacks of September 11, 2001, Wolfowitz was already affirming the necessity of moving to "preemptive war" and directly attacking "rogue states" such as North Korea, Iran and Iraq. It was necessary, he said, to do so without delay, as the disappearance of the Soviet Union gave the United States a great opportunity. He insisted that Washington needn't limit itself to administering crises as they exploded; they could take the initiative, with military means, to redesign borders and reorganize the world.

These are all the ideas of Bush's hawks today, which they tried to make reality after the military victory in April 2003.

TRUE OBJECTIVES OF THE WAR

What legitimacy does this war against Iraq have? What are its true causes? What aims is the Bush Administration pursuing?

The official arguments for the unleashing of the conflict are not convincing. In essence, there are four: 1) Baghdad had not respected 16 resolutions of the Security Council; 2) Iraq held WMD; 3) the Hussein regime committed violations of human rights; 4) it had links to terrorist organizations.

Surrounded by his entourage of hawks and ideologues (who are heavily influenced by fundamentalist religious ideas that verge on the extreme right), President Bush and his cohorts designed the war against Iraq. It had the following objectives:

- To provide a clear response to the attack of September 11, 2001. Public opinion demanded revenge: 70 percent of U.S. citizens believed that Iraq participated in the attacks in some way, and it satisfied them to attack Baghdad. They had not, however, been able to demonstrate that there was the slightest link between Saddam Hussein and Osama Bin Laden.

- To regain control of the Persian Gulf, where two-thirds of the known reserves of oil reside, the key element for the economic growth of developed nations. The attack against Iraq perhaps presages, another attack in the future: against Iran, with the same oil-based objective, but this time looking to the Caspian Sea...

- To establish democracy in Iraq, with the aim of later extending this type of political regime to the entire Middle East.

- To protect Israel against an improbable Iraqi attack, and to continue to foster conditions for a Jewish state in the region, taking it as given that the Palestine question would be resolved with greater ease in a Middle East under the military control of Washington.

THE LOOTING OF BAGHDAD

Under these pretexts, the war took place and the predictable military victory of the U.S. forces and their superfluous British allies followed. We saw on the television screens, with our own eyes, those incredible scenes of looting in Baghdad. In our history courses we had heard about the pillaging of Constantinople in 1204 by the Catholic crusaders; the destruction of Tenochtitlan (Mexico) in 1521 by the Spanish conquistadors; and the sacking of Rome in 1527 by the troops of Charles V. Contemporaries of these crimes, the chroniclers of former times, have left us horrific descriptions of gratuitous murder, large-scale rape, plundering of treasure, demolition of mansions, theft of monuments and arson of palaces.

Arab historians have also given us, with hair-raising detail, descriptions of the other two great devastations of Baghdad: in 1258, at the hands of the Mongols led by Chief Hulagu Khan, who among other barbarities cast the 400,000 volumes of the great library of the university al-Mustansiriya into the Tigris; and again in 1401, carried out by other ferocious Mongols led by the fearsome Tamerlan, "Timur the Lame," who entered the city and annihilated the greatest quantity of material and cultural wealth the world had ever seen.

As we know, this wealthy region of Mesopotamia, the Fertile Crescent in the two valleys of the Tigris and the Euphrates, is considered to be "the cradle of humanity." It is here that the framework of the complex cultures we call civilizations appeared for the first time, 5,000 years before Christ. Here the Akkadian, Sumerian, Babylonian and Assyrian civilizations succeeded each other. Invented here were nothing less than agriculture (the cultivation of sugar cane), cities (Babel), states, writing (cuneiform), law (the code of Hammurabai), monotheistic religion (Abraham was born in Ur), medicine, astronomy, zero and Arabic numerals.

This is the region where the Bible locates heaven on Earth, the Garden of Eden (Genesis 2:14). It is the land of the legendary library of Nineveh, the Tower of Babel and the Hanging Gardens of Babylon, considered by the Greeks to be one of the seven wonders of the world.

Enraged after the invasion of Iraq and the capture of Baghdad, we were witness to monstrous acts of violence — permitted by the U.S. troops — which occasioned the destruction of a great part of the evidence of this glorious past: the pillaging of the Archaeology Museums (in Baghdad, Mosul and Tikrit), the arson of the National Library, the sacking of the Museum of Modern Art, the destruction of the National Conservatory of Music, the arson of the Koranic Library and the sacking of the ruins of Babylon and more than 5,000 archaeological sites.

Thousands of pieces from the Museum of Baghdad were destroyed, and more than 75,000 objects stolen, including some exceptional pieces such as the bronze statue of Basitki, the harp and "The Ram Caught in the Thicket", both from Ur, and the head of the Akkadian king. Among the books from the National Library which burned were *The Canon of Medicine* of Avicena, and *The Treaty on Numbers* of Abu Said Al Maghrebi, which for centuries were the basis of western universities.

This annihilation of part of our own historical memory resulted in the resignation of Martin Sullivan, chair of the Cultural Property Advisory Committee and cultural adviser to George W. Bush, and of Gary Vikan, member of the same committee, because of the passivity of U.S. forces in the face of such acts of barbarism. For Donald Rumsfeld, secretary of defense and the person ultimately responsible for the looting, such disregard for human civilization could be understood as similar to "what happens at a soccer game in England."[6]

THE BUSINESS OF RECONSTRUCTION

The reconstruction of Iraq and the substantial investments this demands have already become the main preoccupations of those who planned the invasion. The war in itself, with its squandering of "intelligent" and "precision" weapons, was already a great deal for certain U.S. weapons manufacturers.

There are six participants who have been the greatest beneficiaries of the destruction of Iraq:[7] United Technologies, which sold weapons worth €4 billion to the Pentagon (such as the Black Hawk and Seahawk helicopters); General Dynamics, €9 billion of weapons (submarines, Abrams tanks, Hydra missiles); Northrop Grumman, €12 billion (aircraft carriers, battleships, F14 Tomcat and F18 Hornet fighter planes, unpiloted Global Hawk aircraft); Raytheon, which also sold €12 billion (Patriot and Tomahawk missiles, BLU109 penetrator bombs); Boeing, €18 billion (Apache and Chinook helicopters, Awacs, B52 and F22 Raptor fighter planes); and Lockheed Martin, €25 billion (F117 invisible aircraft, U2 spy-planes, C130 Hercules).

In total, in the year 2002 the Pentagon prepared for the Iraq conflict by buying €80 billion worth of weapons from these six gigantic companies, a sum which is the equivalent to the annual GNP of a country such as Colombia. Every day, this war cost the United States the astronomical figure of $2 billion. In the first 20 days of the conflict, Washington spent $40 billion or twice the annual value of all the petrol produced by Baghdad, and a greater sum than the Gross Domestic Product (GDP) of Iraq.

Without the slightest twinge of conscience, the weapons companies delighted in this orgy of military spending. Raytheon, for example, the producers of the Tomahawk missiles that punished the civilian population of Baghdad, had seen the value of the shares fall six percent in the beginning of 2003. As soon as Operation "Shock and Awe" began, to the joy of their shareholders, the share value increased more than 16 percent! The business deals don't stop there. The total cost of reconstruction, according to Yale economist William Nordhaus, is estimated at almost $100 billion. The distribution of this enormous pie has made way for a war within the war, between companies and nations who don't want to see themselves excluded from such an extraordinary project.

Washington continues to affirm that the reconstruction will be primarily undertaken by U.S. and British companies. The first lists of firms to benefit — Bechtel Group Inc., Parsons Corp., Halliburton Co., Fluor Corp., — indicate that the government intends to prioritize companies that made the greatest financial contributions to the electoral campaign of George W. Bush, and those that will probably finance his 2004 presidential campaign. They haven't forgotten their buddies either. We have an example of this in those who were to govern Iraq after the fall of Saddam Hussein. The first person Bush named, for a few weeks his proconsul in Baghdad, was ex-General Jay Garner. Garner is a friend to the hawks who planned this war, and also the president of weapons manufacturer SY Coleman, contracted by Raython to make the infamous Patriot missiles so widely used in the conflict.

Another example: to extinguish the oil wells set on fire in the south of Iraq, Kellog Brown & Root was named as the contractor without any previous tendering process. They are a subsidiary to the public works giant Halliburton, whose CEO for many years was current U.S. Vice-President Dick Cheney.

And we should not forget the case of Richard Perle. The press has revealed that Perle, "the Prince of Darkness," fiercely pro-Israeli, chairman of the Defense Policy Board in the Pentagon and one of the men who most wanted the war against Iraq to go ahead, was negotiating important telecommunications contracts in the new Iraq in favor of the company Global Crossing, for which he acts as one of its principal consultants.

JOURNALISTS IN THE WAR

What changes have occurred in terms of the media, if we compare the first Gulf War with the new invasion of Iraq? Essentially, there has been one major change: "embedded" journalists were able to accompany the allied troops to the front line.

The history of the relationship between images and conflicts began in 1854 in the Crimean War, where photographs were taken for the first time. An analysis of the wars which followed — the U.S. Civil War (1861); the Franco-Prussian War (1870); the Boer War in South Africa (1899); World War I (1914); the Spanish Civil War (1936); World War II (1939); the Korean War (1950); the Algerian War (1954); and the Vietnam War (which finished in 1975) — allow us to draw some conclusions.

In particular, we can state the following: democracies that go to war tend to behave differently toward the media, whether we are considering the United States or countries such France and England. The authorities of the latter states, with few exceptions, do not allow journalists to get close to the front lines. They control reports and censor images. They work according to the principle that war is a kind of parenthesis in the life of a democracy, during which certain freedoms — particularly freedom of information — are suspended.

Freedom of information in the United States is inscribed in the constitution. U.S. journalists have been able to express themselves freely and without censorship for this reason. Consider Ernest Hemingway describing the horrors of the trenches of World War I for the *Chicago Tribune*, or photographer Robert Capa disembarking among the GIs on the beaches of Normandy on June 6, 1944. This held true even during the Vietnam War. In that conflict — as Stanley Kubrick showed in the film "Full Metal Jacket" — any accredited journalist held the rank of an official and could move around the war zone at will. They were free to contemplate the darker side of the conflict.

So open was the situation that once the war was lost — the only defeat in the military history of the United States — the Pentagon accused the media of having been the true cause of the U.S. defeat. From that time on it was decided that journalists would never again be authorized to witness combat first hand. Officials specializing in communication would be responsible for sharing information with them in their own way.

The first war fought under these new rules was the Malvinas (Falklands) War in 1982, which was fought between Britain and Argentina. The British created the principle of a journalistic "pool," whereby a select group of journalists committed to share with their colleagues the information they received. No reporters were allowed close to the front lines, but they were overfed "controlled" information. This encouraged the propagation of a version of the war that best served the interests of the military. It is said that the Malvinas War was the first "war without pictures."

Using the same model, the United States carried out the invasion of Grenada in 1983. It was the first U.S. war "without witnesses" in two centuries. The big television networks condemned the Pentagon in the courts for having stopped them from showing this conflict. The Malvinas model of "war without images" was applied again in the invasion of Panama in 1989, the Gulf War in 1991, Kosovo in 1999 and Afghanistan in 2002.

Why has this prudent tradition been interrupted? This decision was made by Donald Rumsfeld, superhawk secretary of defense. At all costs, he wanted the world's journalists to witness the triumphal welcome given to the "liberating" U.S. troops. Instead, for a few surprising days, the "embedded" journalists were witness to the "most modern army in the world" becoming unexpectedly bogged down and the disconcerted reactions of the elite troops.

Five months after the end of the war in Iraq, journalists who were still there bore witness to the general chaos. The incredible incompetence of the occupying forces in terms of administration and public services was displayed, as neither drinking water nor electricity had been fully reestablished. An atmosphere of great insecurity still prevailed. Attacks multiplied, as much against U.S. and British troops as against foreign embassies, the local headquarters of the United Nations (twice), Shi'ite dignitaries and governing council members. At the beginning of September 2003, the troops had already suffered as many casualties in the period following the conflict as during the conflict itself.

This chaos and the tragic lack of preparation for peace have led a growing number of analysts to question the methods used by President Bush and his advisers as they convinced public opinion of the necessity of this war. What has been discovered leaves one aghast.

LIES OF STATE

It's like the story of the thief who yelled "Stop, thief!" The dossier against Saddam Hussein that President George Bush presented to the UN General Assembly on September 12, 2002, was called *A Decade of Lies and Deceit*. And what did he offer for proof? A flood of lies. Essentially, he claimed that Iraq had close links with the al-Qaida network and that it was a threat to the security of the United States because it possessed "weapons of mass destruction" — a terrifying phrase invented by Bush's media advisers.

We now know that these claims, widely challenged at the time,[8] were indeed false. It is becoming ever clearer that the U.S. Administration manipulated the information about Iraq's WMD capabilities.

The 1,400-strong inspection team of the Iraq Survey Group, under General Dayton, has still not found the slightest scrap of evidence. And we have now found out that at the time Bush made these charges, he had already received reports from his security services proving them false.[9] According to Jane Harman, a Democrat congresswoman from California, we have been the victims of the "biggest cover-up of all time."[10] For the first time in its history, the U.S. public is questioning the true reasons for a war, although only now that the conflict is over.

A key role in the massive deception was played by a secret department at the Pentagon's heart, the Office of Special Plans (OSP). As revealed by veteran journalist Seymour M. Hersh in the *New Yorker* on May 6, 2003,[11] the OSP was established by Paul Wolfowitz, number two at the defense department, and headed by a noted hawk, Abram Shulsky. The OSP's mission was to analyze data received from U.S. security services — the CIA, the Defense Intelligence Agency (DIA), the NSA (National Security Agency) — and produce summaries for the government. Relying on reports from Iraqi exiles closely linked to the Pentagon-financed Iraqi National Congress, and its president, the questionable Ahmad Chalabi, the OSP overinflated both the threat of the WMD and the links between Saddam Hussein and al-Qaida.

Scandalized by these manipulations, a group of former experts from the CIA and the State Department, who have called themselves "Veteran Intelligence Professionals for Sanity" issued a memorandum to President Bush on May 29, 2003. They claimed that information "had been falsified in the past, for political reasons, but never in such a systematic way designed to mislead our elected representatives into authorizing a war."[12]

It is also clear that even the U.S. Secretary of State Colin Powell was manipulated, and his political future is now at stake. He is reported to have resisted pressure from the White House and the Pentagon to distribute the more dubious briefings. Prior to his famous speech to the UN Security Council on February 5, 2003, Powell was obliged to read a draft prepared by Lewis Libby, chief of staff to Vice-President Dick Cheney. It contained such doubtful information that Powell is said to have become angry, thrown the sheets in the air and declared, "I won't read that. That's s..."[13] Finally, Powell requested that the head of the CIA, George Tenet, sit in view behind him to share responsibility for what was being read.

In an interview in the June 2003 issue of *Vanity Fair*, Paul Wolfowitz admitted that lies of state had been told. He said that the decision to put forward the threat of WMD to justify preemptive war against Iraq had been adopted "for reasons that have a lot to do with U.S. Government bureaucracy." For the core reason, he stated, "We settled on the one issue which everyone could agree on, which was weapons of mass destruction."[14]

In this way, the war to topple the Baghdad regime, take hold of Iraqi oil and remodel the Middle East was launched. WMD and the links with al-Qaida were mere pretexts.

BLAIR AND AZNAR AS ACCOMPLICES

The president of the United States lied. Searching desperately for a casus belli to bypass the United Nations and rally some accomplices (such as the United Kingdom and Spain), Bush did not hesitate before inventing one of the greatest lies of state ever.

He was not the only one. Speaking before the House of Commons in London, his ally the British Prime Minister Tony Blair (soon to be tarnished by the Kelly affair), said on September 24, 2002, "Iraq possesses chemical and biological weapons... Its missiles can be deployed in 45 minutes."[15] Donald Rumsfeld, U.S. secretary of state, affirmed in January 2003, "There is no doubt in my mind that the Iraqis have chemical and biological weapons."[16] In his presentation to the UN Security Council on February 5, 2003, Colin Powell declared, "Saddam Hussein has investigated dozens of biological agents causing diseases such as gas gangrene, plague, typhus, tetanus, cholera, camel pox and hemorrhagic fever."[17] And finally, U.S. Vice-President Dick Cheney, on the eve of the war in March 2003, claimed,

"We believe that Saddam Hussein has actually rebuilt nuclear weapons."[18]

Throughout his innumerable speeches, President Bush has hammered home these accusations. In a radio-transmitted speech to the nation on February 8, 2003, he went as far as supplying the following details: "Iraq has sent bomb-making and document forgery experts to work with al-Qaida. Iraq has also provided al-Qaida with chemical and biological weapons training. And an al-Qaida operative was sent to Iraq several times in the late 1990s for help in acquiring poisons and gases."[19] The warmongering mass media, transformed into distributors of propaganda, repeated these denunciations ad nauseum, on the Fox, CNN and MSNC television networks; through the radio broadcaster Clear Channel (1225 stations in the United States), and even in the prestigious newspapers such as the *Washington Post* and the *Wall Street Journal*. Throughout the world, these false accusations have constituted the principal argument of the war-hungry.

The arguments were also repeated by each of Bush's allies. Let's begin with the most zealous among them, Spanish President José María Aznar, who declared to the Court of Madrid on February 5, 2003, "We all know that Saddam Hussein has weapons of mass destruction... Equally, we all know that he holds chemical weapons."[20] Carrying out Bush's command a few days earlier, on January 30, 2003, Aznar had drawn up a declaration of support for the United States known as the "Letter of 8." It was signed by Tony Blair, Silvio Berlusconi and Vaclav Havel, among others. In this document they affirmed that the "Iraqi regime and its weapons of mass destruction represent a clear threat to world security."[21]

On March 16, 2003, three days before the beginning of the war, Bush, Blair, Aznar and Duraõ Barroso (prime minister of Portugal), declared that Saddam Hussein's refusal to get rid of his nuclear, chemical and biological weapons and his long-range missiles paved the way for a military attack.

PROPAGANDA MACHINES

Thus for more than six months, to justify a preemptive war that neither the UN General Assembly nor world public opinion wanted, the doctrinaire sect surrounding Bush have spread their lies of state with a presumptuousness more befitting the most hated regimes of the 20th century, through a veritable machine of propaganda and indoctrination. They have joined the long tradition of lies of state which have punctuated the history of the United States. One of the most sinister of these concerned the destruction of the U.S. battleship, the *Maine*, in Havana Bay in 1898. This served as the pretext for the United States to enter into the war against Spain, and led to the annexation of Cuba, Puerto Rico, the Philippines and the island of Guam.

On the night of February 15, 1898, at around 9.40 p.m., the *Maine* was the victim of a violent explosion. The ship sank in Havana Bay and 260 men perished. Immediately, the popular press accused the Spanish of having placed a mine below the hull. The press denounced their barbarism, their "death camp" and even their cannibalistic practises. Two media magnates led the rivalry in the search for the sensational: Joseph Pulitzer, of the *World,* and William Randolph Hearst, of the *New York Journal.* This campaign received the support of U.S. businessmen who had made large investments in Cuba, and dreamed of ousting Spain from the territory. But the public showed hardly any interest. In January 1898, the cartoonist for the *New York Journal,* Frederick Remington, wrote to his boss from Havana: "There is no war. Request to be recalled." Remington's boss, William Randolph Hearst, sent a cable in reply: "Please remain. You furnish the pictures, I'll furnish the war."[22]

As can be seen in "Citizen Kane," the film by Orson Welles (1941), Hearst mounted a violent campaign. For several weeks, following February 15, day after day, Hearst dedicated several pages of his newspapers to the *Maine* affair, demanding vengeance as he unceasingly repeated, "Remember the Maine! To hell with Spain!" All the other newspapers followed. The distribution of the *New York Journal* grew from 30,000 to 400,000 copies, then regularly sold more than one million copies! Public opinion reached a white heat. The atmosphere was staggering. With pressure on all sides, President William McKinley declared war on Madrid on April 25, 1898. Thirty years later, in 1911, an inquest into the destruction of the *Maine* concluded that there had been an accidental explosion in the engineroom.[23]

In 1960, in the middle of the Cold War, the CIA distributed to a few journalists some "confidential documents" which demonstrated that the Soviets were on the way to winning the arms race. Immediately, the mass media began to pressure the presidential candidates, clamoring for a substantial increase in defense loans. Harassed, John F. Kennedy promised to devote billions of dollars to the relaunching of the program to build cruise missiles to bridge the missile gap. This is precisely what was hoped for, not only by the CIA, but also by the military-industrial complex. Once he was elected and the program was voted in, Kennedy discovered that the military superiority of the United States over the Soviet Union was overwhelming.

In 1964, two destroyers were claimed to have been attacked in the Tonkin Gulf by North Vietnamese torpedoes. Immediately, the media made it a national affair. They cried humiliation and demanded reprisals. President Lyndon B. Johnson used these attacks as a pretext to launch retaliation bombings against North Vietnam. He demanded a resolution from Congress allowing him to engage the U.S. Army. And so commenced the Vietnam War, which only ended — in defeat — in 1975. Later it was learned, from the mouths of the crews on the two destroyers in question, that the attack in the Tonkin Golf had been pure invention.

A similar scenario occurred with President Ronald Reagan. In 1985, Reagan suddenly declared a "national emergency" because of the "Nicaraguan threat" represented by the Sandinistas in power in Managua. The Sandinistas, let us note, were elected democratically in November 1984, and they allowed both political freedoms and freedom of expression. Nonetheless, Reagan affirmed, "Nicaragua is two days' driving time from Harlingen, Texas. We are in danger!"[24] Secretary of State George Schultz stated before Congress, "Nicaragua is a cancer which insinuates itself in our territory. It applies the doctrines of *Mein Kampf* and threatens to take control of the whole hemisphere."[25] These lies of state justified the massive aid given to anti-Sandinista rebels, the "Contras," and led to the Iran-Contra scandal.

We won't elaborate on the lies of the Gulf War of 1991, analyzed at length[26] and remaining in our memories as paradigms of modern brainwashing. Facts constantly repeated, such as: "Iraq, the fourth largest army in the world"; "the pillaging of the Kuwaiti maternity wards"; "the unbreakable defensive line"; "surgical strikes"; "the efficiency of the Patriot missile" etc., all revealed themselves to be totally false.

MANIPULATING PUBLIC OPINION

After the controversial victory of George W. Bush in the U.S. presidential elections of November 2000, the manipulation of public opinion has become a central concern of the new administration. After the attacks of September 11, 2001, this concern was transformed into a veritable obsession. Michael K. Deaver, friend of Donald Rumsfeld and specialist in "psywar" (psychological warfare) techniques, claimed that from here on in military strategy needed to be thought of in terms of television coverage. He stated that with public opinion, the war effort was unstoppable, but without it, Washington was powerless.

From the beginning of the war against Afghanistan, in coordination with the British Government, "Coalition Information Centers" were established in Islamabad, London and Washington. Genuine propaganda offices, they were conceived of by Karen Hughes, media adviser to Bush, and, above all, by Alistair Campbell, Blair's powerful political image guru. A spokesperson for the White House explained the centers' role: "The television networks continuously broadcast information, 24 hours a day; so, these centers will provide them with information 24 hours a day, seven days a week."[27]

On February 20, 2002, the *New York Times* unveiled the most fantastic manipulation project yet. To direct the "war of information," the Pentagon obeyed the instructions of Donald Rumsfeld and the Sub-Secretary of Defense Douglas Feith and secretly created the Office of Strategic Influence (OSI). It was placed under the management of Air Force General Simon Worden, with the mission of spreading false information to benefit the cause of the United States. The OSI was authorized to practise disinformation, particularly with regard to foreign media. The *New York Times* specified that the OSI had signed a contract of $100,000 per month with a communication enterprise, the Rendon Group. This group had been employed in 1990 in the preparation of the Gulf War, and had developed the false declaration of the "nurse" who claimed to have seen Iraqi soldiers pillaging the Kuwait Maternity Hospital. According to her, "They took the babies out of the incubators, took the incubators and left the babies on the cold floor to die."[28] This eyewitness accountant was instrumental in convincing the members of Congress to vote in favor of the Gulf War.

Officially out of action after the revelations of the press, the OSI has certainly continued to be active. If not, how can some of the grosser manipulations of the recent war in Iraq be explained? Let us especially consider the enormous lie told about the spectacular liberation of soldier Jessica Lynch.

"SAVING PRIVATE LYNCH"

You will remember the beginning of April 2003, when the U.S. mass media broadcast, with an impressive wealth of detail, the facts of Jessica's story. She was one of a group of 10 U.S. soldiers captured by Iraqi forces. Trapped in an ambush on March 23, she had resisted to the end, firing on her attackers until she ran out of ammunition. She was finally stabbed, tied up and taken to a hospital in enemy territory, at Nassiriya. A week later, U.S. special forces helicoptered in to free her, in a surprise operation preceded by sustained fire and explosions. Despite the resistance of the Iraqi guards, the commandos managed to penetrate the hospital, take hold of Jessica and take her to Kuwait by helicopter.

That very night, President Bush announced the liberation of Jessica Lynch to the White House and then to the nation. A week later, the Pentagon distributed to the media a video filmed during the exploit, with footage worthy of the better caliber of war movies.

But the conflict in Iraq ended on April 9, and a certain number of journalists — particularly those from the *Los Angeles Times,* the *Toronto Star, El País* and BBC World — went to Nassiriya to verify the Pentagon version of events regarding Jessica's liberation. They were bitterly disappointed. According to their interviews with the Iraqi doctors who had cared for the young woman[29] — a version of events confirmed by the U.S. doctors who had seen her after her "deliverance" — Jessica's wounds (a broken arm, a broken thigh and a dislocated ankle) were not due to gunfire, but were caused by the accident which happened to the truck she was traveling in. She was not mistreated. On the contrary, the Iraqi doctors had done everything possible to care for her. "She had lost a lot of blood," recounted Dr. Saad Abdul Razak, "and we had to give her a transfusion. Luckily, some members of my family have the same blood group as she does, O-positive. We could get sufficient quantities of blood. Her heart rate was 140 beats per minute when she arrived here. I think we saved her life."[30]

Taking insane risks, these doctors tried to contact the U.S. Army to restore Jessica to them. Two days before the intervention of the special commandos, they had even driven their patient close to U.S. lines in an ambulance. But the soldiers opened fire on them and almost killed their own heroine.

At dawn on April 2, special commandos equipped with an impressive panoply of sophisticated weapons surprised the staff of the hospital. Two days before, the Iraqi doctors had informed the U.S. forces that the Iraqi Army had withdrawn and that Jessica was waiting for them. Dr. Anmar Ouday described the scene to John Kampfner of the BBC: "It was like a Hollywood film. They cried 'go, go, go,' with guns... without bullets, [with] blanks and the sound of explosions. They made a show for the American attack on the hospital — action movies like Sylvester Stallone or Jackie Chan."

These scenes were filmed with a night vision camera operated by a former assistant to Ridley Scott on the film "Black Hawk Down" (2001). According to Robert Scheer of the *Los Angeles Times*, the images were immediately sent for editing to the central command of the U.S. Army in Qatar. Once they were assessed by the Pentagon, they were broadcast to the entire world.[31]

The story of the liberation of Jessica Lynch will remain in the annals of war propaganda. In the United States, it will perhaps be considered the most heroic moment of the conflict, even though it has been proven to be an invention as fake as that of the WMD supposedly held by Saddam Hussein, or the links between the former Iraqi regime and al-Qaida.

Drunk on power, Bush and his entourage have misled the U.S. people and world public opinion. According to Professor Paul Krugman, their lies constitute "the worst scandal in American political history, worse than Watergate, worse than Iran-Contra."[32]

ANOTHER WORLD IS POSSIBLE

From one end of the planet to the other, deprived of a voice and alternatives for too long, more and more citizens are clamoring "Enough!" Enough of accepting neoliberal globalization as our fate. Enough of letting the market supplant our democratically elected representatives. Enough of seeing our world put up for sale. Enough of putting up with this situation, being resigned and giving in.

Bringing together dozens of NGOs, collectives, associations, unions and networks from numerous countries, an embryo of international civil society has begun to take shape.

Throughout the 1990s, the phenomenon of globalization and the laxity of political leaders brought about deep changes in the structures of power. The real lords of the Earth are no longer those who exhibit the trappings of political power, but those who control the financial markets, the media groups of worldwide reach, the information highways and genetic technologies. Under the supervision of this ersatz planetary surveillance council, a kind of world board of directors or de facto world government has been established, with the IMF, the World Bank, the OECD and the WTO as the key players.

Following the example of the once hyper-industrialized states like the Soviet Union, huge private groups today exploit the environment with their disproportionate resources, stripping nature of the riches that are the heritage of all humanity. They have no scruples and no limits. Wherever they go, they exacerbate the ecological crisis, multiplying already-intense levels of pollution, speeding up the greenhouse effect, extending desertification, causing the "black tides" of enormous oil slicks, and propagating new pandemics (HIV/AIDS, the Ebola virus, Creutzfeldt-Jakob Disease, etc.).

Indifferent to democratic debate and immune to universal suffrage, these unofficial powers are the de facto governors of the planet. They have the supreme power to decide the destiny of the world's inhabitants without any countervailing power that could rectify, amend or reject their decisions. The traditional counterbalancing powers — parliaments, political parties and the mass media — are either too local or too heavily implicated. In these circumstances, most of us have some idea that we need a countervailing power, based in international civil society, that could stand up to this planetary executive.

In taking up the banners of international protest once again, today's rebels — those who have spoken out in Seattle, Washington, Prague, Davos, Quebec, Genoa, Barcelona and Porto Alegre — have begun to construct this countervailing power. In some way, they are trying to lay the foundations for a new sphere of world representation, at the center of which would be international civil society.

The generalized commodification of words and objects, of bodies and minds, of nature and culture, has only exacerbated existing inequalities. Although the production of basic foodstuffs worldwide fulfills more than 110 percent of the planet's needs, 30 million people continue to die of hunger every year, and more than 800 million are suffering from malnutrition. In 1960, the richest 20 percent of the world's population earned 30 times more than the poorest 20 percent. Today the rich are earning 82 times more. Of the six billion inhabitants of the planet, barely half a billion are comfortably off, while 5.5

billion suffer hardship. More than 1.2 billion people, or a fifth of humankind, have less than a euro per day to clothe and shelter themselves, to move around, to care for themselves and to eat.

Is it so surprising, then, that the demand for justice and equality — always present in the background of humanity's long history — should have made such a forceful reappearance in our own times? This is especially so when new dangers are continuing to appear.

The concentration of power and capital has been extraordinarily accelerated over the last 20 years because of the revolution in information technologies, and the fact is that the new genetic techniques for manipulating life also herald a huge leap forward at the start of this millennium.

This is still more evident after the announcement in Washington on June 26, 2000, that the human genome, in other words, the three billion nucleotide bases or the basic links of our genetic makeup, had been almost totally deciphered. Researchers are now studying the tens of thousands of genes contained in DNA, the constituents of the biological memory of our species and the foundation of medicine for the future. When we get to know their functions, we can obtain new medicines and new forms of gene and cellular therapy. This prospect is revolutionizing the strategies of the pharmaceutical industry and heralds ethical and commercial controversies. A new El Dorado for "post-genomic" investors, our very genes represent today a source of potentially substantial profits for those who have deciphered them.[1]

Commercial exploitation of the human genome and the generalized patenting of life open up yet more prospects for the expansion of capitalism. Faced with these new threats, citizens are claiming a new generation of rights. After demanding their political and then their social rights, this time they want their collective rights: the right to the conservation of nature, the right to a nonpolluted environment, the right to the city, the right to peace, the right to information, the right to childhood, the right to development for all peoples of the world.

It seems incredible now that this incipient civil society is not better represented in the large-scale international negotiations. It is here
that major issues are discussed, concerning the environment, health,
the sway of finance, humanitarianism, cultural diversity, genetic
manipulation, etc.

If we want to change the world, we need to think about how to
construct a different future. We can no longer accept the fact that one
billion people of the planet live well while the other five billion are
forced to survive in conditions of appalling wretchedness.

These five billion citizens are represented every year at the World
Social Forum in Porto Alegre, simply an assembly of the peoples of
the world. This is the first time that people from everywhere have
decided to meet in one place to speak out about how they are suffering
because of neoliberal globalization. Represented by thousands of
associations and NGOs, it is a meeting place for people who are
humiliated, who do not have a roof over their heads, who lack medicine, work, or water to drink and who are not respected by their own
political leaders.

Porto Alegre is a gathering of the socially excluded — those who
have been cast aside and condemned by globalization. It is a totally
innovative event. They are discovering that they can get together,
and that there is happiness in being together. They are also discovering that their coming together is amazing and that it is impressing
the world. They are frightening for the owners of the world, to whom
they have given a list of claims that are indispensable if they are to
escape from the horror of their economic circumstances.

The time has come to found a new, more caring economy, one
based on the principle of sustainable development, where the human
being is of central concern. The first step is to disarm the power of
finance.

In the last two decades, economic ultraliberalism has not ceased
to shrink the political domain and alarmingly reduce the boundaries
of democracy. The dismantling of financial power requires significant

taxing of capital gains and, particularly, speculative transactions on the exchange market (the Tobin Tax).[2] It is also essential to boycott and to abolish tax havens, those zones governed by banking secrets that cover up the misappropriations and other crimes of the finance mafia.

We shall also have to design a new distribution of work and income within a plural economy. In this economy, the market occupies only one part, there is a sector concerned with solidarity, and more and more time is made for leisure.

The establishment of an unconditional and universal basic income, conceded to each individual from birth, independent of family or professional status, obeys the revolutionary principle that every human being has the right to this vital salary. We all deserve it, not so much to stay alive, as for the simple reason of being alive. The introduction of this salary is based on the idea that the productive capacity of a society is the result of all the scientific and technical knowledge that has been accumulated by previous generations. This unconditional basic income would be the individual legacy of this collective heritage. It could be extended to everyone in the world, because what the world produces today, equally distributed, would be sufficient to guarantee adequate conditions of life for all the inhabitants of the planet.

To this end, we must return the poor countries of the South to their proper place in the world. This means putting an end to policies of structural adjustment; annulling most of their official debts; increasing development aid; accepting the fact that they may not choose to adopt the ecologically nonsustainable model of the rich countries; promoting economies based on the resources of each country; fostering fair trade; making huge investments in education, housing and health; demanding protection for indigenous minorities; providing access to drinkable water for the 1.5 billion people who are lacking it; bringing in laws for the general protection of the environment; and establishing, especially in the developed world, regulated social and environmental protections on imported products, so that proper working conditions for unwaged workers in the underdeveloped world could be guaranteed.

Other urgent additions are necessary if this program is to change the world: the International Criminal Court; the emancipation of women on a planetary scale; the creation of an international authority to guarantee that citizens could be free from the lies told and propagated by the mass media; the establishment of the principle of foresight and prevention with regard to the environment and, especially, genetic manipulation. Once utopian ideals, these dreams have become the specific political objectives of this new 21st century.

ACRONYM LIST

ABM: antiballistic missile
AC!: Act Together Against Unemployment (*Agir Ensemble Contre le Chômage*)
Act Up: AIDS Coalition to Unleash Power
ANC: African National Congress
ASPA: American Service Members Protection Act
ASEAN: Association of Southeast Asian Nations
ATTAC: Action for a Taxation of Financial Transactions to Aid Citizens (*Action pour une taxation des transactions financières pour l'aide aux citoyens*)
CIA: Central Intelligence Organization
CTBT: Comprehensive Test Ban Treaty
DAL: Right to Housing (*Droit au Logement*)
DIA: Defense Intelligence Agency
ETA: Basque Fatherland and Liberty (*Euzkadi Ta Askatasuna*)
FARC: Revolutionary Armed Forces of Colombia (*Fuerzas Armadas Revolucionarias de Colombia*)
FBI: Federal Bureau of Investigation
FN: National Front (*Front National*)
G7: Group of Seven (France, the United States, Britain, Germany, Japan, Italy and Canada)
G8: Group of Eight (G7 with the addition of Russia)
GATT: General Agreement on Tariffs and Trade
GDP: Gross Domestic Product
GMO: Genetically Modified Organism
GNP: Gross National Product

ICC: International Criminal Court
ICCY: International Criminal Court for the former Yugoslavia
ILO: International Labor Organization
IMF: International Monetary Fund
IRA: Irish Republican Army
IUCN: World Conservation Union (International Union for the Conservation of Nature and Natural Resources)
KVM: Kosovo Verification Mission
NAFTA: North American Free Trade Agreement
NATO: North Atlantic Treaty Organization
NGO: Nongovernmental Organization
NSA: National Security Agency
OECD: Organization for Economic Cooperation and Development
OSCE: Organization for Security and Cooperation in Europe
OSI: Office of Strategic Influence
OSP: Office of Special Plans
PLO: Palestine Liberation Organization
PT: Brazilian Workers' Party *(Partido dos Trabalhadores)*
SLA: South Lebanon Army
TNP: Treaty of Non-Proliferation
UÇK: Kosovo Liberation Army *(Ushtria Clirimtare E Kosoves)*
UNAIDS: Joint UN Program on HIV/AIDS
UNHCR: United Nations High Commission for Refugees
UNICEF: United Nations International Children's Emergency Fund
WEF: World Economic Forum
WHO: World Health Organization
WMD: Weapons of Mass Destruction
WSF: World Social Forum
WTO: World Trade Organization

NOTES

CHAPTER ONE

1. *International Herald Tribune*, Paris, January 7, 2002.
2. Madeleine Albright, former secretary of state to President Clinton, went so far as to assert, for example, that CNN was the "16th member" of the UN Security Council.
3. The euro (€) was introduced in 2002 as the common currency within the European Union. It is used by the majority of EU nations. At the time of writing, US$1 was approximately equal to €0.85. — Eds.
4. The total goods and services production of a country.
5. cf. Ignacio Ramonet, *La tiranía de la comunicación* (Madrid: Debate, 1998).
6. cf. "Ravages des technosciences," *Manière de voir*, N° 38, Paris, March-April, 1998.
7. B. Ward, (New York: W. W. Norton & Co, 1964).
8. Donella H. Meadows, (New York: Universe Books, 1972).
9. IUCN UNEP WWF, (Gland, Switzerland: IUCN, 1980).
10. *Our Common Future: The World Commission on Environment and Development,* Bruntland, G. (ed.), (Oxford, Oxford University Press: 1987).

11. cf. Ricardo Petrella, *Économie sociale et mondialisation de l'économie* (Montreal: Suco Éditeur, 1997).

12. Kris Dechouwer, "Unité et diversité de l'extrême droite européenne," *Politique*, N° 21 in "Extrême droite en Europe" (Brussels: November 2001); see also, Gilles Ivaldi, ed., "L'extrême droite en Europe occidentale," *Problèmes politiques et sociaux*, N° 849, La Documentation française, Paris, December 22, 2000.

13. *Le Monde*, Paris, April 13, 1996.

14. Both parties bring together individuals of different sensibilities: Catholics, traditionalists, those who yearn for the good old days of the Vichy regime, veterans of the Organisation Armée Secrète still wanting a French Algeria, monarchists, racists, neopagans, etc.

15. cf. Mark Hunter, *Un Américain au Front. Enquête au sein du FN*, (Paris: Stock, 1998).

16. *Le Monde*, Paris, December 30, 2001.

17. Sofres, *L'État de l'opinion 1991* (Paris: Le Seuil, 1991).

18. François Furet and Stéphane Courtois, et al. (Harvard: Harvard University Press, 1999).

19. *Libération*, Paris, March 20, 1998.

20. cf. Klaus Mann, *Le Tournant* (French translation by N. Roche), (Paris: Solin, 1984), p.329 ff.

21. Cambridge: Polity Press, 2001.

22. London: Blackwell, 2000.

23. In France, the "plural left" government of Lionel Jospin sponsored several important laws that represent undeniable social advances: youth employment, the 35-hour week, universal health cover (CMU) and personalized subsidies for the self-employed (APA).

24. cf. Roland Hureaux, "Les trois âges de la gauche," *Le Débat*, Paris, January 1999.

25. cf. Pierre Bordieu, "L'essence du néolibéralisme," *Le Monde diplomatique*, Paris, March 1998; see also, by the same author, "Le néolibéralisme, utopie (en voie de réalisation) d'une exploitation sans limites," in *Contre-Feux* (Paris: Liber-Raison d'Agir, Vol. I, 1998).

26. Only mass education movements (Ligue de l'enseignement, Foyers

Léo-Lagrange, Foyers ruraux, etc.) have a global vision like that of the parties: that of educating all citizens.

27. See *Porto Alegre (Foro Social Mundial 2002): Una asamblea de la humanidad* (Barcelona: Icaria, Más Madera Collection, 2002).

CHAPTER TWO

1. cf., Alain Gresch, *Israël, Palestine: La vérité sur un conflit* (Paris: Fayard, 2001).

2. *La Repubblica*, Rome, September 18, 2001.

3. *El Mundo*, Madrid, September 29, 2001.

4. Cited by Jean-Claude Buisson in Emmanuel de Waresquiel (ed.), *Le Siècle rebelle: dictionnaire de la contestation au XXe siècle* (Paris: Larousse, 1999).

5. *El País*, Madrid, November 10, 2001.

6. *Le Monde*, Paris, November 30, 2001.

7. *El Mundo*, Madrid, June 1, 2002.

8. *Le Monde*, Paris, June 8, 2002.

9. *International Herald Tribune*, Paris, December 1, 2001.

10. Hundreds of suspects, accused of belonging to al-Qaida and of having fought with the Taliban, were moved to the U.S. base of Guantánamo in Cuba, in early January 2002.

11. For example, *Newsweek*, New York, November 5, 2001.

12. Quoted by *El País*, Madrid, November 7, 2001.

13. *Le Monde*, Paris, December 14, 2001.

14. *El País*, Madrid, May 29, 2002.

15. cf. François Heisbourg, *Hyperterrorisme: la nouvelle guerre* (Paris: Odile Jacob, 2001). See also Pascal Boniface, *Les Guerres de demain* (Paris: Le Seuil, 2001).

16. After September 11, perhaps we should ask if it is reasonable to go ahead with the construction of the future giant Airbus. This ecological

aberration, with the capacity the carry 1,000 passengers, would evidently constitute an appalling weapon in the hands of a mad pilot.

17. However, the attacks have made it clear that dams and nuclear power plants are not immune from the attacks of plane-bombs.

18. Washington immediately understood the significance of the challenge, and attempted to respond — in my view erroneously — by prohibiting any images of bodies being shown, so as not to give those behind the crimes the further satisfaction of contemplating the most tragic aspect of the vulnerability of the United States.

19. To such a point that *Time* magazine, greatly scandalizing the straitlaced members of the U.S. public, had been considering naming Osama Bin Laden as 2001 "person of the year." They eventually opted for Rudolph Giuliani, the mayor of New York.

20. cf. Ignacio Ramonet, *La tiranía de la comunicación*, *op. cit.*, particularly the chapter entitled "Mesianismo mediático" ("Media Messianism").

21. *Le Monde*, Paris, November 3, 2001.

22. The base of Pearl Harbor, attacked on December 7, 1941, is in Hawaii, at that time a colony of the United States.

23. See Paul-Marie de La Gorce, "Controverses à Washington," *Le Monde diplomatique*, Paris, November 2001.

24. *International Herald Tribune*, Paris, November 21, 2001.

25. *Ibid.*, November 24, 2001.

26. *Ibid.*, January 7, 2002.

27. *Ibid.*, November 24, 2001.

28. "Democracy stood still for a moment after September 11 in the United States and Europe," declared Freimut Duve, representative for freedom of the press in the OSCE, *Le Monde*, Paris, November 7, 2001. See also, Patti Waldmeir and Brian Groom, "In Liberty's Name," *Financial Times*, London, November 21, 2001.

29. *International Herald Tribune*, Paris, November 21, 2001.

30. See, *inter alia*, the interview with Kofi Annan, *Le Figaro*, Paris, November 5, 2001; *Financial Times*, London, November 21, 2001; *El País*, Madrid, November 19, 2001; and the interview with Joseph E. Stiglitz, Nobel Prize for Economics, *Le Monde*, Paris, November 6, 2001.

31. See Ignacio Ramonet, *Geopolítica del caos* (Madrid: Debate, 1999).

CHAPTER THREE

1. On October 19, 2000, the UN High Commission for Refugees (UNHCR) condemned Israel for its "disproportionate use of force against innocent and unarmed civilians," describing the treatment of the Palestinian civilian population by the Israeli army as a "war crime."

2. See Ammon Kapeliouk, "Yenín, encuesta sobre un crimen de guerra," *Le Monde diplomatique en español,* Valencia, May 2002.

3. Alain Joxe, "Israël entre en guerre civil," *Le Monde,* Paris, October 19, 2000.

4. The average Palestinian salary per capita has notably declined, dropping from $2,245 in 1992 to $1,940 in 1999. In 1999, the unemployed represented 19.7 percent of the economically active population of the West Bank, and 27.3 percent in Gaza, but these figures increased by as much as a third again with the Israeli army blockade.

5. According to a Gallup poll published in the newspaper *Maariv* on November 5, 2001, 53 percent of Israelis are in favor of negotiating a definitive peace agreement. See also Dominique Vidal, "La clé palestinienne," in *Manière de voir,* N° 60, "11 septembre 2001: Ondes de choc," Paris, November-December 2001.

6. *Haaretz,* Tel Aviv, 25 January 1998.

7. It is a dreadful and paradoxical fact that Israel is the last place in the world where Jews are killed for the simple fact of being Jewish.

8. cf. Dominique Vidal, *La Peché original d'Isräel: L'expulsion de Palestiniens revistée par les "nouveaux historiens" israéliens,* new expanded edition (Paris: L'Atelier, 2002).

9. Alexis de Tocqueville, *El Antiguo Régimen y la Revolución* (Madrid: Alianza Editorial, 1982).

10. cf. Éric Rouleau, "En Iran, islam contre islam," *Le Monde diplomatique,* Paris, June 1999.

11. See also Alain Gresh, *Israël-Palestine: La vérité sur un conflit, op. cit.*

12. Ilan Pappé, *The Making of the Arab-Israeli Conflict, 1947–51* (New York: I.B. Tauris, 1992).

13. *Le Monde*, Paris, January 9, 2001.

14. *Ibid.*, December 29, 2000.

15. See, also Alain Gresch, "Proche-Orient, la paix manquée" and "La proposition israélienne sur les réfugiés palestiniens à Taba," *Le Monde diplomatique*, Paris, September 2001.

16. *Jeune Afrique*, Paris, February 24, 1998.

17. *Le Monde*, Paris, February 16, 1997.

18. *Ibid.*, September 27, 1996.

19. In regard to this conflict, the obsession about balance and equality of treatment, seems to have controlled the mass media, as a contrast to the prevailing norm established in the wars of the Gulf, Rwanda, Somalia, Bosnia, Kosovo, Chechnya and Afghanistan. This norm was the crudest form of Manicheism: "Saddam Hussein is Hitler," or "Milosevic is Hitler." As reprehensible as that Manicheism was then, it is equally irrational now to call for balance in a situation that is manifestly unbalanced. The military superiority of Israel is overwhelming from any point of view. The words of Jean-Luc Godard are pertinent here: "Democratic debate disgraces itself when it is conceived of as, 'one minute for Hitler, one minute for the Jews.'"

20. *Le Monde*, Paris, November 8, 2000.

21. cf. Gilles Paris, "La Palestine en miettes," *Le Monde*, Paris, October 20, 2000.

22. Edward W. Said, "Israël-Palestine: pour une troisième vie," *Le Monde diplomatique*, Paris, August 1998.

CHAPTER FOUR

1. David S. Landes, *L'Europe technicienne* (Paris: Gallimard, 1975), p.214.

2. cf. Ignacio Ramonet, *La tiranía de la comunicación, op. cit.*

3. *Business Week*, New York, February 14, 2000.

4. *Le Monde*, Paris, March 12, 2000.

5. Carlos Gabetta, *La Debacle de Argentina* (Barcelona: Icaria, 2002).

6. *Le Monde*, Paris, January 3, 2002.

7. cf. André Gorz, *Misères du present, richesse de l'avenir* (Paris: Galilée, 1997).

8. cf. François Chesnais, *La Mondialisation du capital*, new expanded edition (Paris: Syros, 1997).

9. *Libération*, Paris, October 15, 1997.

10. In order to avoid accusations of favoring the reconstitution of "natural monopolies," the U.S. Government filed a formal complaint against Bill Gates' company Microsoft on May 18, 1998, for breaking antitrust laws.

11. François Chesnais, *La Mondialisation du capital, op. cit.*, p.215.

12. *Ibid.*, p.253.

13. Louis Villermé, *Tableau de l'état physique et moral des ouvriers.* [1840] (Paris: Edhis, 1989).

14. Cited by Jacques Droz in *Histoire générale du socialisme* (Paris: PUF, "Quadrige" collection, Vol. I, 1997), p.369.

15. Karl Marx, *Manifiesto comunista* (Barcelona: Crítica, 1998).

16. cf. Claire Briset, *Un monde que dévore ses enfants* (Paris: Liana Lévi, 1997).

17. cf. Bernard Schlemmer, *L'Enfante exploité* (Paris: Khartala, 1996). See also the dossier "L'Enfante exploité." *Page 2*, N° 2, Lausanne, June 1996.

18. *Rapport mondial sur le développement humain* 1997 (Paris: Economica, 1997).

19. See Mahbub Ul Haq, Inge Kaul, Isabelle Grunberg, *The Tobin Tax: Coping with Financial Volatility* (Oxford: Oxford University Press, 1996).

20. For further information, consult the Forum website (www.forum-socialmundial-org.br). See also *Porto Alegre (Foro Social Mundial): Una asamblea de la humanidad* (Barcelona: Icaria, 2002).

21. Pepa Roma, *Jaque a la globalización: Cómo crean su red los nuevos*

movimientos sociales y alternativos (Barcelona: Grijalbo, Arena Abierta collection, 2001).

22. See the dossier "Comment l'OMC fut vaincue," *Le Monde diplomatique*, Paris, January 2000.

23. *International Herald Tribune*, Paris, February 2, 2000.

24. Joseph S. Nye, Jr. "Take Globalization Protest Seriously," *ibid.*, November 25, 2000.

25. Cited by Jean-Paul Maréchal in *Humaniser l'économie* (Paris: Desclée de Brouwer, 2000), p.22.

26. Miguel Benasayag and Diego Sztulwark, *Du contre-pouvoir* (Paris: La Découverte, 2000).

27. Bernard Cassen, "Démocratie participative à Porto Alegre," *Le Monde diplomatique*, Paris, August 1998.

CHAPTER FIVE

1. See the complete document (in English) of the Rambouillet Agreement at the *Le Monde diplomatique* website (*www.monde-diplomatique.fr*).

2. cf. Richard Holbrooke, "El mayor fracaso colectivo de Occidente," *Política exterior*, Madrid, January-February 1998.

3. Catherine Samary, "La resistible dislocation du puzzle yougoslave," *Le Monde diplomatique*, Paris, July 1998.

4. Warren Zimmerman, *Origins of the Catastrophe: Yugoslavia and its Destroyers* (New York: Times Books, 1996).

5. Noel Malcolm, *Bosnia: A Short History* (New York: New York University Press, 1994).

6. *International Herald Tribune*, Paris, May 18, 1999.

7. *Le Figaro*, Paris, May 3, 1999.

8. cf. Ignacio Ramonet, *La tiranía de la comunicación, op. cit.*

9. cf. William Branigin, "U.S. Detailed Serb Terror in Kosovo," *International Herald Tribune*, Paris, May 12, 1999.

10. cf. Régis Debray, "Une machine de guerre," *Le Monde diplomatique*, Paris, June 1999.

11. cf., *inter alia*, Edgar Morin "Le désastre," *Le Monde*, Paris, April 23, 1999; François Maspero, "Kosovo: le crime annoncé," *Le Monde*, Paris, April 24, 1999; Jean Daniel, "Le sens d'un combat," *Le Nouvel Observateur*, Paris, April 22, 1999.

12. *Le Monde*, Paris, March 25, 1999.

13. *Ibid.*, February 19, 1999.

14. cf. William Pfaff, "What Good is NATO if America Intends to go it Alone?" *International Herald Tribune*, Paris, May 20, 1999.

15. *Ibid.*

16. William J. Perry, "La construction d'alliances par le leadership global et la dynamique d'enlargement" (speech given March 4, 1996), *Cahiers d'études strategiques, N° 20*, Paris, Spring 1997.

17. cf. Jean Radvanyi, "Sale guerre en Tchétchénie," *Maniére de voir, N° 49*, "L'Atlas 2000 des conflicts," Paris, January 2000.

18. *Le Monde*, Paris, May 22, 1999.

19. The three issues that led to the conflict between Rome and Carthage in the 3rd and 4th centuries BC.

20. In the end, the British legal system permitted Pinochet to return to Chile for health reasons.

21. Alain José, "Le nouveau statut des alliances dans la stratégie américaine," *Cahiers d'études stratégiques, N° 20*, Paris, Spring 1997.

22. An International Security Assistance Force, approved by the Bonn Agreements and with troops from 17 countries, initially sent 3,500 men to Kabul and its surroundings with the aim that the force should eventually be deployed throughout Afghanistan.

CHAPTER SIX

1. Jean Delumeau and Yves Lequin (eds.), *Les Malheurs des temps* (Paris: Larousse, 1987).

2. This has been guaranteed since 1995 by the Treaty of Non-Proliferation (TNP), which recognizes the five permanent members of the UN Security Council — China, the United States, France, the United Kingdom and Russia — as the only authorized nuclear powers of the planet. Cuba, India, Israel and Pakistan are the only countries that have not subscribed to it.

3. Declaration made at the *Institut des hautes études de la défense nationales* in Paris, October 22, 1999.

4. cf. *Transversales Science Culture*, January-February 1999.

5. *Le Temps*, Geneva, November 24, 1999.

6. *Le Monde*, Paris, June 17, 1999.

7. Jean-Yves Nau, "Brevets industriels pour matériau humain?," *Le Monde*, Paris, July 22, 2000.

8. See *The Economist*, New York, July 1, 2000.

9. A videogame in the range of Nintendo's Game Boy products, along with cartoon films and collectable cards, Pokémon and its myriad sub-products invaded the world at the end of the 1990s and spread like wildfire. Coined from the words "pocket monster," Pokémon refers to a range of mutating fantasy creatures, gnomes of the biotechnological era, creatures that live in the grass, undergrowth, woods, caves, lakes, etc. There are about 150 in total, all different and each with its own particular genetic makeup. Some are very rare and others very difficult to capture. The point of the game is that the Pokémons have to be caught. They then have to be domesticated and trained so they can then mutate into another species. They metamorphose, change their appearance or, in a word, "evolve" (the Darwinian concept is part of the game) and develop new abilities, new powers, etc. In this age of the biotechnological revolution, cloning and invasions of GMOs, is it really surprising that children are so taken with the idea of "friendly mutants"?

10. Antonin Artaud, *El teatro y su doble* (Barcelona: Edhasa, 1997).

11. Extremely contagious, foot-and-mouth disease was described in the 16th century and its virus was identified in 1898. It is not, however, lethal for stock, with less than five percent mortality rate. Throughout its history, Europe has known dozens of epizootic epidemics of foot-

and-mouth disease. In the past, however, some weeks after contracting the disease, the animals recovered and the quality of the stock was restored.

12. *Daily Mail*, London, March 1, 2001.

13. *International Herald Tribune*, Paris, March 16, 2001.

14. *Le Monde*, Paris, March 13, 2001.

15. *Ibid.*, September 28, 2000; *L'Expansion*, Paris, March 5, 2001.

16. cf. Olivier Godard, "De la nature del principe de précaution," in Edwin Zaccaï and Jean Nöel Missa (eds.), *Le Principe du précaution: Significations et conséquences* (Brussels: Éditions de l'Université de Bruxelles, 2000).

17. A higher death toll than for traffic accidents, which accounted for 8,487 deaths in 1999.

18. Both of them social evils, two legal drugs claim even more victims in France. Alcohol is responsible for 42,963 deaths and tobacco 41,777 deaths (1997 figures).

19. Between 1975 and 1995, with the increasing use of garbage incinerators, the number of cancer cases in France went up by 21 percent in men and 17 percent in women.

20. As early as 1923, Rudolph Steiner, the controversial personality who inspired biodynamic agriculture, warned against the dangers of making bovine animals carnivorous. *Le Monde,* Paris, May 6, 1996.

21. *http://www.unhchr.ch/udhr/index.htm, Article 25.1.*

22. Address: 4, rue Niepce, 75014 Paris, France (e-mail: str@acf.imaginet.fr).

23. Sylvie Brunel and Jean-Luc Bodin, *Géopolitique de la faim: Quand la faim est une arme…* Annual report of *Action contre le faim* (Paris: PUF, 1998).

24. *El País*, Madrid, October 16, 1998.

25. *Le Monde*, Paris, November 26, 1999.

26. *Le Monde*, Paris, December 2, 1999.

CHAPTER SEVEN

1. *http://www.un.org/Docs/journal/asp/ws.asp?m=S/RES/1441(2002).*

2. *Op. cit.*

3. *Op. cit.*

4. *http://abcnews.go.com/sections/world/dailynews/terror_980609.html*

5. *http://usinfo.state.gov/topical/pol/usandun/bushun912.htm*

6. *http://www.ananova.com/news/story/sm_785556.html*

7. *http://www.worldpolicy.org/projects/arms/updates/081203.html*

8. See also: Ignacio Ramonet, "De la guerre perpétuelle," *Le Monde diplomatique*, Paris, March 2003.

9. See also: *International Herald Tribune*, Paris, June 14, 2003 and *El País*, Madrid, June 1 and 10, 2003.

10. *Libération*, Paris, May 28, 2003.

11. *http://www.commondreams.org/views03/0506-06.htm*

12. *http://www.counterpunch.org/vips02082003.html*

13. See: *International Herald Tribune*, Paris, June 5, 2003.

14. *http://www.scoop.co.nz/mason/stories/WO0305/S00308.htm*

15. *http://www.pbs.org/newshour/updates/iraq_09-24-02.html*

16. *Time*, New York, June 9, 2003.

17. *http://www.state.gov/secretary/rm/2003/17300.htm*

18. *Time*, New York, June 9, 2003.

19. *http://usinfo.state.gov/regional/nea/iraq/text2003/0208bush.htm*

20. *El País*, Madrid, June 4, 2003.

21. *http://www.caabu.org/press/documents/euro-letter-times.html*

22. *http://www.smplanet.com/imperialism/remember.html*

23. *http://www.herodote.net/histoire02151.htm*

24. *http://www.reagan.utexas.edu/resource/speeches/1986/30386a.htm*

25. See also: "Interview with Noam Chomsky," *Télérama*, Paris, May 7, 2003.

26. See particularly: Ignacio Ramonet, *La Tyrannie de la communication* (Gallimard, col. Folio actuel, n°92: Paris, 2001).

27. *The Washington Post,* Washington, November 1, 2001.

28. See: *http://www.globaled.org/curriculum/cm18a.html.* This fake nurse was the daughter of the Kuwaiti ambassador to Washington at that time. Her false testimony had been conceived and scripted by Michael K. Deaver for the Rendon Group. Deaver was the former assistant to the president and deputy chief of staff to President Reagan.

29. BBC, London, May 18, 2003 *http://news.bbc.co.uk/2/hi/programmes/ correspondent/3028585.stm*

30. *El País,* Madrid, May 7, 2003.

31. BBC, London, May 18, 2003 *http://news.bbc.co.uk/2/hi/programmes/ correspondent/3028585.stm*

32. *Los Angeles Times,* Los Angeles, May 20, 2003. See also: *http://www.robertscheer.com/*

CHAPTER EIGHT

1. *Le Monde,* Paris, June 17, 2000.

2. This is the aim of the international association ATTAC — *www.attac.org*

ALBERT EINSTEIN
Edited by Jim Green

Hailed as a scientific genius, harassed by the FBI as a subversive for his socialist views.

ISBN 1-876175-63-X

HELEN KELLER
Edited by John Davis

Revolutionary activist, better known for her blindness than her radical social vision.

ISBN 1-876175-60-5

HAYDÉE SANTAMARÍA
Edited by Betsy Maclean

Woman guerrilla fighter in the Cuban Revolution, whose passion for art and politics inspired the Latin American cultural renaissance.

ISBN 1-876175-59-1

radical history

CHILE: THE OTHER SEPTEMBER 11
Reflections on the 1973 Coup
Edited by Pilar Aguilera and Ricardo Fredes

An anthology reclaiming September 11 as the anniversary of Pinochet's U.S.-backed coup in Chile, against the government of Salvador Allende. With essays by Ariel Dorfman, Victor Jara, Pablo Neruda and many more.

ISBN 1-876175-50-8

POLITICS ON TRIAL
Five Famous Trials of the 20th Century
By William Kunstler
Introduction by Michael Ratner, Karin Kunstler Goldman and Michael Smith

William Kunstler, champion of civil liberties and human rights, reflects on five famous cases in which ordinary citizens were targeted for the color of their skin or the views they held.

ISBN 1-876175-49-4

ONE HUNDRED RED HOT YEARS
Big Moments of the 20th Century
Preface by Eduardo Galeano
Edited by Deborah Shnookal

A thrilling ride through the 20th Century: 100 years of revolution, reaction and resistance.

ISBN 1-876175-48-6

GLOBAL JUSTICE
Liberation and Socialism
Ernesto Che Guevara

Is there an alternative to the neoliberal globalization ravaging our planet? Collected here are three classic works by Che Guevara, presenting his radical view of a different world based on human solidarity and understanding.

ISBN 1-876175-45-1

CAPITALISM IN CRISIS
Globalization and World Politics Today
Fidel Castro

Cuba's leader adds his voice to the growing international chorus against neoliberalism and globalization.

ISBN 1-876175-18-4

WAR, RACISM AND ECONOMIC INJUSTICE
The Global Ravages of Capitalism
Fidel Castro

Including Cuba's first response to 9/11 and the war on Afghanistan, Fidel Castro analyzes the crisis of the Third World, the possibilities for sustainable development and the future of socialism.

ISBN 1-876175-47-8

MANIFESTO
Three Classic Essays on How to Change the World
Ernesto Che Guevara, Rosa Luxemburg, Karl Marx and Friedrich Engels

"Let's be realists, let's dream the impossible." Che Guevara's words summarize the radical vision of the four famous rebels presented in this book: Marx and Engels' *Communist Manifesto*, Rosa Luxemburg's *Reform or Revolution* and Che Guevara's *Socialism and Humanity*.

ISBN 1-876175-98-2